MYSTERIOUS
NORTHUMBERLAND

MYSTERIOUS
NORTHUMBERLAND

RUPERT MATTHEWS

breedon **books**
PUBLISHING

First published in Great Britain in 2009 by
The Breedon Books Publishing Company Limited
Breedon House, 3 The Parker Centre,
Derby, DE21 4SZ.

ISBN 978-1-85983-677-4

Printed and bound by TJ International Ltd, Padstow, Cornwall.

CONTENTS

Introduction   7

1 Mysterious Elementals & Devils   9

2 Mysterious Little People   20

3 Mysterious Treasures   48

4 Mysterious History   67

5 Mysterious Ghosts   110

6 Mysterious Witches   147

7 Mysterious Beasts   164

8 Mysterious Saints   174

9 Mysterious Crimes   185

Index   191

INTRODUCTION

Northumberland is a border county, where the land always seems to be on a strangely indefinable edge.

Few counties in England have borders as clearly drawn as those of Northumberland. To the east spread the restless waters of the North Sea, covering a drowned land of long forgotten valleys, hills and plains. The sea has lashed the Northumbrian coast with storms since time immemorial and across its waters have ventured invaders and raiders. The sea has also provided a living for generations of fishermen and traders, merchants and sailors, who have braved the foam and its mysteries.

To the south the county ends on the banks of the Tyne, that great river of the North East. The twin branches of the North Tyne and South Tyne come tumbling down from the soaring heights of the Cheviots and Pennines respectively, joining at Hexham to form the mighty torrent that runs through Tynedale and Newcastle upon Tyne to reach the sea at industrial Tynemouth. The river has never been tamed and even today is liable to burst its banks in devastating floods if heavy rains lash the uplands from where it originates.

Those high hills and mountains form the western border of Northumberland. They are at once a barrier and a safeguard, for beyond the Cheviots lies Scotland. For centuries the border raiders came and went, raiding both sides of the border whether there was peace or war between the kings of England and Scotland. There are mysteries enough among these hills and valleys to last anyone for many years.

To the north the county ends on the Tweed. Like the Tyne, the Tweed rises on the inland hills, but unlike the Tyne it reaches deep into Scotland and only its lower stretches form the northern boundary of Northumberland, and of England. This river, too, can flood with devastating ease, sweeping a vast mass of water down the valley to brush aside the works of mere man.

Within those borders, Northumberland is one of the most sparsely populated counties in England. Outside of the Newcastle-Tynemouth conurbation there are said to be more sheep than men. Whether or not that is true, vast swathes of the county are indeed dominated by sheep and the rough grazing on which they thrive. Moors and windswept heather hillsides stretch on for mile after mile in the higher parts of the county. The lowlands and coastal plain are astonishingly fertile and productive by comparison, dotted with villages and farms that offer a warm hospitality typical of the county.

So much of the county is built upon its rocks that they can not be ignored. Limestone, sandstone and millstone grit form the western uplands, yielding a poor soil too barren for the plough. The lowlands are built on softer rocks that have weathered gently to produce a fertile soil that has long been farmed – as shown by the huge numbers of prehistoric monuments that dot the landscape. Then there is the enigmatic Whin Sill, a band of enormously hard rock that slashes across the county from the Farne Islands through Bamburgh and Housesteads to reach the Cheviots. Millions of years ago this was the site of a vast volcano of truly awesome power. The magma it spewed out can be found scattered across some 350 square miles, but it is the solid ridge of the Whin Sill where it is most obvious.

It was because Northumberland sat on the border between Scotland and England that this land was kept wild, untamed and thinly populated for far longer than the rest of England. In 1521, when the constant border feuding was perhaps at its height, there were over 200 fortified buildings in the county. These ranged from the vast edifices of Alnwick and Bamburgh Castles, through to the border watching posts known as bastles that overlooked all the routes between the two kingdoms, down to the pele towers and thickly walled houses that served to protect life and limb of more humble families when the Scots came pouring over the border to loot, kill and pillage.

Normal everyday agriculture could not be carried out with the constant threat from the Scots, so human life was few and far between. Where people did not tread, the land was far from empty. It was here that dragons stalked the land, that ghosts drifted intent on their lonely missions beyond the grave and that the enigmatic and often dangerous fairy folk wandered. They wander still, if the stories are to be believed. The wild Northumberland countryside is not just a borderland between two human kingdoms, but also between this world and the other world. It is here that the boundary between our rational human world of science and technology and the other world of phantoms and spirits is remarkably thin.

There is something about Northumberland that is inherently mysterious. It cannot be touched or pinned down, and some miss it altogether. However, for those who are able and willing to pause and look about themselves, the magical and the supernatural are never far away. There is much to gaze at in Northumberland, be it the splendours of urban Newcastle or the wild, remote heights of the Cheviots. Everywhere there is something odd and mysterious, sometimes caught in the corner of the eye but which vanishes as soon as it is searched for.

This truly is the most mysterious of English counties.

CHAPTER I

MYSTERIOUS ELEMENTALS & DEVILS

The wilder areas of Northumberland do not often feel the tread of a human. But it was not always so.

In days gone by, before the advent of off-road landrovers and quadbikes that can whisk men up to the sheep pastures in minutes, shepherds used to walk the hills on foot in all but the very worst winter weather. These men knew that the hills were not empty, that much older creatures than they stalked the uplands and were best left well alone. Some said that they were the evil angels swept out of heaven by St Michael after the rebellion of Satan against God, others that they were the little people who had lived in the hills before humans came to the land, but whoever they were the shepherds knew to treat them with respect and to avoid them whenever possible.

The most dangerous of all these little folk were to be found on the Simonside Hills. These towering heights dominate the southern side of Coquetdale west of Rothbury. Simonside itself rises to 1,409 feet and presents a dramatic and rugged face to the world. It dominates the scene, although the neighbouring Tosson Hill is actually some 40 feet taller. These hills are covered with heather, gorse and bracken as well as rough grazing for the sheep.

Some years before the railways came to the area, two young men of some wealth came out of Newcastle to enjoy a week or so of hunting up in the hills. They chose the Simonside Hills for their expedition. After obtaining lodgings in Rothbury – at the time something of a health resort for the gentry from the industrial cities – they set off up into the hills with their guns. Around noon they stopped for a bite to eat and a drink in a quiet green opening in the heather and gorse on the upper slopes of Simonside.

Suddenly, a short man dressed all in brown clothes the same shade as dry bracken stepped into the open space. The odd figure had a broad, muscular chest and stout arms. His head was topped by a wild mop of red hair and his eyes bulged unnaturally. The short man seemed to be as surprised to see the young men as they were to encounter him.

'Do ye know who I am?' the newcomer demanded belligerently.

Thinking that it would be best to be polite, the younger of the two Newcastle men replied that he took the short man to be the lord of the manor. The short man grunted, but continued to glare at the two hunters. The younger man then said that he would be willing to hand over the game birds that they had shot, if the lord of the manor so wished.

The dwarf shook his head, declaring that he did not eat flesh. He preferred, he said, to eat whortleberries, cloudberries, mushrooms and nuts in the summer, while feasting on crab apples, plums and sloes in the winter. He finished by asking if the two young men would like to join him for a meal. The younger man was all for accepting but the older of the two stammered out a polite refusal and dragged his friend off down the hill toward Rothbury. There was, he said, something about the dwarf that had upset him.

When the two men got back to Rothbury they told their landlord about the 'little brown man' that they had met. They were surprised that their tale evinced no surprise, but that instead the locals declared the men wise to refuse the invitation. The claim to be vegetarian was false, it appeared, for the dwarves of Simonside were notorious for eating any humans who they could entice into entering their lair and turning their backs, even for a moment.

Some years earlier a shepherd from a county to the south came to Rothbury to work on the Simonside Hills. One chill evening, soon after he began work, the man was faced by an uncomfortable night in the open with only his thick woollen cloak to keep him warm. At that moment he saw a light as if from a cottage window flickering some distance off. Climbing up a hillside, the man saw a small hut and knocked. There was no answer so the shepherd pushed the door open to find a small room with a warm fire burning in the grate and a lantern on the window sill. A bundle of chopped firewood lay beside the fire and a pair of mighty logs lay on the floor as if waiting to be cut up.

The Simonside Hills are home to a disturbingly violent race of elemental entities, much given to feasting on human flesh.

The man seated himself down on one of the two stones that obviously served as fireside stools and waited for the owner. When the door eventually opened in stepped a short, stout man clad all in brown. The dwarf eyed the man coldly, then without a word sat down on the other stone stool. Realising that he must have inadvertently entered the home of one of the dwarves of which he had been warned, the man sat stock-still. He knew that the rigid rules of hospitality meant that he was safe so long as he sat in the dwarf's house, but he feared greatly what might happen if he left. He decided to do nothing to offer offence.

The hours passed with the man sitting unmoving and worried, while the dwarf lounged easily and ignored his visitor. The fire slowly died down as the chill wind got up and the temperature plummeted. Eventually the man could keep still no longer. When the dwarf appeared not to be looking the man picked up a few pieces of firewood and tossed them on to the flames.

The dwarf shot the man a look of the utmost contempt. He bent down to pick up one of the great logs, casually snapped it in half over his knee and tossed one half on to the flames.

Now seriously alarmed, the shepherd sat upright and wide awake, determined to see in the dawn when he might be able to make a run for it over the heather. When dawn eventually did come it brought with it not only the thin, grey light of the rising sun but also the sudden and spectacular disappearance of both the dwarf and his hut. The man found himself sitting in the open air with the cold ashes of the fire stirring in the breeze at his feet. Just inches away to his right was a sheer cliff dropping 100 feet to the rocks below. Realising what a close escape he had had, the man fled home to the south.

In the early 19th century a traveller came to Rothbury who was educated and had no time for tales of the supernatural. He recalled that he had once entered a haunted wood with a superstitious local. The ghost had appeared, shrieking its malevolence and causing the local to flee. However, he had stood his ground and soon saw the 'ghost' to be nothing more paranormal than an owl. He declared that the supposed dwarves of Simonside were nothing more than wild fowl and animals seen in the half light by terrified and imaginative locals. To prove it, he went up to the hills one evening clad in a thick overcoat and armed with a stout staff.

As dusk came on the man saw what looked like a lantern gleaming from a cottage window a short distance away over the heather. Warily he set off toward it, and was soon grateful for his caution. The path he was following suddenly disappeared into a dark, wet bog. The man assumed that it was the locals playing a trick on him and called out to them. The light at once went out. It was replaced by a scurrying noise as if several small creatures were moving rapidly through the heather. The man had no doubt that these were the animals and fowl he had held responsible for the old tales so he lashed out with his stick.

The stick struck something solid, and a small man no more than three feet tall leapt from the heather yelping in pain. The man stared in amazement at the dwarf, but not for long. Flaming torches could be seen moving over the hillside. The dwarf yelled out a threat and a curse, whereupon the flaming torches began moving toward them. The dwarf glared in undisguised hatred at the human intruder and pulled a club from his belt.

Without waiting to see any more, the man fled. He bounded down the hillside, stumbling over roots and falling into the heather as he ran and tripped and ran again. Behind him he could hear the dwarves shouting and could see the torches moving to and fro over the heather-clad slopes. Eventually he got back to Rothbury and soon left to return to the certainties of his home.

Such are the more commonly told tales of the cannibalistic Simonside dwarves. Some sceptics are tempted to dismiss the stories as being nothing more than folklore or legend, but most legends have some sort of basis in fact. This raises the question as to whether the magical and legendary Little Brown Men really did exist in some form.

The key features of the Little Brown Men on which nearly all stories agree is that they live up on the Simonside Hills, that they are dangerous and that they are very strong and cunning — perhaps even eating their human victims. There are two theories about how these tales may have come about. The first, and most popular, dates the origin of the Little Brown Men to the lawless days of the mediaeval border wars. Outlaws and refugees may have sought sanctuary up in the hills, living as outcasts and preying on their more settled neighbours. That such temporary communities or bands of desperate men did exist is beyond doubt, and they may well have survived in popular imagination as the Little Brown Men.

Rather more daring scholars wonder if the Little Brown Men might date back even further. While the behaviour of the Simonside dwarves may fit what is known about mediaeval outlaws, their physical description and way of life does not. After all, a mediaeval refugee was no more likely to be short, muscular and dark than anyone else in Northumberland. However, the description of a tribe of people who are short, dark and wear distinctive clothes does match a group of people who did once live in Northumberland.

Before the English arrived, the land was home to a mix of peoples. Some were Celts, others were of much older stock and it is perhaps these ancient Britons who lie behind the Simonside tales. The pre-Celtic peoples have been shown by archaeology to have been shorter than more recent arrivals to Britain. Early stories of the Celts indicate that these people were not only short but dark and swarthy as well. If a tribe of such people were to survive long enough to meet the English, then they would have done so only in a remote and underpopulated region that was not coveted by the Celtic farmers. The bleak, windswept Simonside Hills are just such a place.

Of course, the tales of the Little Brown Men may be nothing more than stories. However, it is likely that they are based on something. The mysterious folk who lived in Britain in prehistoric times would seem to fit the bill. Perhaps they did survive up in the hills in small numbers to fairly recent times. Perhaps they live there yet.

Another relic from days gone by is the terrifying man and his equally horrific entourage who are said to ride out over the hills and moors north of Haltwhistle. This is the Wild Hunt, which may be encountered by the unwary at almost any spot across England but its favoured runs are these hills and consequently are the most often used.

The Wild Hunt rides only at night and all that most folk know of it are its unnerving sounds, which are very similar to those of a fox hunt undertaken by humans. The carrying cry of a horn will echo out through the darkness, followed by the deeper baying of hounds. Those with any sense will head for hiding at this point, but those who are unable to find cover may find that as the Wild Hunt grows closer it is accompanied by the yelping of dogs and the dull pounding of horses' hooves on turf.

Those few humans who have seen the Wild Hunt and lived report that it is led by a pack of hunting hounds. These dogs are larger than foxhounds and jet black in colour. Their mouths hang open, slavering with froth, while their eyes are large and round and seem to glow with an inner fire. Behind the great hounds come the riders. They are tall men dressed all in black astride tall black horses. Sparks flash from the horses' hooves as they strike the ground and the men's eyes flash with fire. The huntsman is the most impressive figure of them all. Dressed in the most magnificent clothes of the finest cut and bedecked with jewels, he is tall, handsome and truly terrifying.

Just who these men are and what they are hunting is a matter of some mystery. The most common explanation is that they are the minions of Satan sent to ride the world in search of the souls of the damned. Some believe that the lead huntsman is the Devil himself, others that he is a senior demon such as Beelzebub. Other versions do not identify the huntsmen with hell but agree that the quarry of the Wild Hunt are those evil humans who deserve to be torn to pieces by a hellish pack of hounds. A few hold that the Wild Hunt is merely after human prey, no matter if the person in question has led a wicked life or not.

One thing is for certain: nobody is going to be foolish enough to halt the Wild Hunt and ask them their business. Those who have seen this great apparition have usually done so from the cover of a ditch or hedge, but according to local legend one farmer, a century or so ago, was bolder. Having drunk more than was good for him on market day, the man encountered the Wild Hunt as he walked home. The hounds and riders swept past him in a tumultuous rush, and as the huntsman himself approached, the drunken farmer called out.

'Hey,' he cried. 'Have you had good hunting this night?'

The huntsman dragged his jet black stallion to a halt and grinned down at the swaying farmer.

'Aye,' he glowered. 'We have had good sport.' With that he threw a bundle of rags down to the ground. Then with a shout of laughter the huntsman spurred off in pursuit of his men and dogs. The farmer bent down to unwrap the bundle to find that it contained the corpse of his own baby son.

The oldest mention of the Wild Hunt comes in a chronicle that was kept in Peterborough in 1127. Although the account is almost 900 years old, all the essential features of the Wild Hunt are present: 'Many people both saw and heard a whole pack of huntsmen in full cry. They straddled black horses while their hounds were pitch black with staring, hideous eyes. This was seen in the very park of Peterborough town and in all the wood stretching from that spot as far as Stamford. All through the night monks heard them sounding and winding their horns. Reliable witnesses declared that there might well have been 20 or even 30 of them in this wild pursuit.'

Research has shown that the early Christians used the beliefs of the pagans against them. Modern traditional celebrations linked to Christmas, for instance, preserve the customs and beliefs of our pagan predecessors. Some researchers have no doubt that the Wild Hunt is a direct reference to one of the most important and savage gods of the pagan English: Woden.

This great god was the magician of the English deities. It was he who hung himself upside down from the World-Tree to gain wisdom and who imparted some of that wisdom to humans. He ordered human societies, cared for warriors and led the gods into battle. One of his chief pleasures was to lead the 'furious army' through the skies at night to search the world for his enemies. The description that the pagans gave of this furious army may sound familiar. The army rode black horses, dressed in black armour and were led by the commanding figure of Woden on his great black horse with eight legs, Sleipnir.

Whether the Wild Hunt is truly Woden and his furious army is not clear. Woden is not depicted as having any hounds riding ahead of his force, but perhaps he has collected them over the last few centuries. It may be that the Wild Hunt is led by Satan, or it might have some other origin entirely different. Whatever the truth, it is best to stay out of the way when the Wild Hunt comes riding by.

Another tall, dark and savagely handsome man who once rode the highways of Northumberland was the wicked Sir Guy de Ville of Lowick Moor. As with the Little Brown Men and the Wild Hunt, it is generally assumed that Sir Guy de Ville had some sort of origin in reality, although his story as it has come down to us seems more linked to magic and the paranormal than to the ordinary world. His very name 'de Ville' has been taken as a clue to this man's true identity: the Devil.

The story states that at some indeterminate time in the later Middle Ages a man calling himself Sir Guy de Ville came riding into Lowick. Behind him rode a band of savage, fully armed men and a coach groaning under the weight of the vast treasure of gold that it contained. Sir Guy bought a great stretch of land and built himself a pele tower, a fortified home that was common in the troubled Border regions. Into this grand house he moved with his squad of armed men.

Sir Guy never provided any explanation as to where he had come from, where he had got his money from nor why he had chosen Lowick to be his home. Rumours and gossip soon filled in the gaps. A passing traveller said that he recognised Sir Guy as the leader of a band of mercenaries who had been active in Spain. Another reported that the mercenaries had hired themselves out, not only to the highest bidder, but had even fought for the Moslem Moors of southern Spain against the Christian lords of the north. Speculation was rife that Sir Guy had learned the dark arts of sorcery from his Moorish masters.

Lowick Moor is today a quiet area grazed by sheep, but not so long ago the Devil himself stalked the moors.

Another traveller passing through said that he though Sir Guy was, in reality, Sir Guy Somerville. The Somervilles were a wealthy and respectable family from the Scottish lowlands. This Sir Guy had vanished as a young man some 10 years earlier after his family had disowned him and thrown him off their estates. In truth, however, nobody really knew who Sir Guy de Ville really was.

What did soon become clear, however, was that he was a man of unbridled lusts and passions who had a bottomless pocket and a band of equally violent armed men to back him up. The trouble began as drunken escapades. Sir Guy and his men would start fights, smash up property and behave in the most base and violent manner to their neighbours. When none of the local farmers lifted a finger against Sir Guy and his murderous colleagues, the rogues grew bolder. Men and women were whipped for saying the wrong thing, children were thrashed for no reason at all. From the day he had arrived, Sir Guy had shown himself to be obsessed with women. He spent his money freely to seduce local girls or to hire in women of loose morals from Newcastle. Soon the rapes began, with husbands being held at swordpoint by the wicked knight's henchmen.

After three years of this wild, lawless behaviour, Sir Guy de Ville was found lying dead on the outskirts of Woodend Forest. His neck was broken. His band of brutal followers was gone and his pele tower pillaged and empty. Nobody knew what had happened. Perhaps his own men had killed him for his money. Perhaps a wronged husband had battered de Ville to death, after which the cut-throats had fled. Anybody who knew was not telling.

The good vicar of Lowick then had a problem. It was his duty to bury all Christians, no matter how wicked their deeds had been. It was not for him to decide if such men were worthy of divine forgiveness or not. However, Sir Guy de Ville was different. If he had fought for the Moslems and dabbled in sorcery, could he be deemed to be a Christian at all? After much debate the funeral went ahead. It was well attended, for the local folk wanted to make sure that Sir Guy was dead.

Dead or not, Sir Guy did not stay buried for long. Within a month his ghost was seen galloping over Lowick Moor. The area was soon subjected to a wide range of paranormal activity. Lady Barmoor of Barmoor Castle was awoken by the ghost of Sir Guy, and a few nights later Lord Barmoor woke to find his wife gone.

A gigantic white hare was seen running over the moors, but no hunter was ever fast enough to catch it. Hares have traditionally been linked to witchcraft and sorcery, so this hare was at once taken to be a manifestation of Sir Guy. One local hunter, Watty Diccon, decided to make silver bullets for his musket by melting down coins. The next time he saw the white hare he let fly with his special ammunition and scored a hit. The white hare tumbled over in the heather but ran off at high speed. At dawn the next day Lady Barmoor was found dead on her doorstep with a silver bullet lodged in her heart.

Following this, the body of Sir Guy was exhumed and found to be as fresh as the day it was buried. The corpse was burned and the ashes scattered into a nearby stream. And yet, Sir Guy could not rest. His wicked spirit is supposed to ride over Lowick Moor to this day. As with the Wild Hunt, it is best to dive for cover when you hear the sound of hoofbeats.

It is difficult to know what to make of this tale. There are no historic records of a Sir Guy de Ville owning land in the area, but that does not mean anything much. Before peace came with the union of the crowns of England and Scotland in 1603 this was a wild place. In any case, Sir Guy may have merely rented his lands and pele tower and so his name may not have been recorded.

The story as we have it was first recorded in something like this form in the mid-19th century. It clearly falls into two parts. The events ascribed to Sir Guy when he was alive are cruel and wicked, but perfectly human. There is no reason why some wild young man, born of a good family, should not go abroad to earn a living as a mercenary and then return with his riches and savage temper. The events believed to have happened after Sir Guy's death, on the other hand, are clearly repeating motifs and are found in many folk tales, legends and stories that have little or no grounding in fact.

The best guess as to the origins of the story of Sir Guy de Ville of Lowick is that it grew out of real events. A vicious and unpleasant stranger probably did move into the Lowick area, though whether his name was as suggestive as de Ville is unlikely. No doubt he did come to a sudden and violent end. Thereafter the tales of hares, ghosts and the like probably gathered around his memory until all that was left was a folktale.

Another local celebrity who may have existed in reality is the Cresswell Tailor. According to local stories this man lived sometime around the 1750s. He was the best tailor in all Northumberland, and, according to himself, the best in England, but his business never prospered because of his fondness for drink. When he should have been working, he was drinking. When he should have been at market buying cloth, he was boozing in the taverns. When he should have been impressing clients, he was lying drunk in their kitchens.

One evening the tailor was in the local tavern and, as was usual when he was drunk, was boasting about his skills and the fine gentlemen for whom he had worked. The locals, knowing his quarrelsome nature when in his cups, were loudly agreeing with him. However, there was a stranger in the inn that night; a stranger dressed in fine clothes of a dark colour and foreign style. He sat quietly eating his meal and taking no notice of the boastful tailor.

The tailor spotted the man and took umbrage at his refusal to appreciate his boasts. The tailor's boasts got louder and more outrageous. He claimed to have made the favourite hunting coat of the Duke of Northumberland, which was true, and to have clothed the Duke's son Lord Percy in a velvet court suit, which was also true. Then he boasted of how he would make clothes for the king and his princes, of how he could make a coat fit for an emperor. Finally, he declared that he could make a coat for the Devil. Still the well-dressed stranger said nothing. He got up quietly, paid his bill and left.

Some time later the drunken tailor left the inn to weave his way home. As he staggered over the great green at Cresswell, the tailor came across the stranger. The well-dressed man smiled at the tailor. 'So,' he said in a silken voice heavy with menace. 'You say that you can make a coat for the Devil do you, my man?' Suddenly nervous, the tailor nodded. 'Very good,' the stranger continued, 'then make me a coat. And if it is as good as your boasts I will pay you well. But if it is faulty I will have your body and soul.' The stranger chuckled, then held out his arms for the suddenly very sober tailor to measure him up. When the measuring was completed, the stranger bowed low to the tailor. 'I will return here in a week', he said in his soft terrifying tones. 'Make sure my coat is ready.' With that he strode off into the dark woods beyond Cresswell Tower.

The village of Cresswell was once home to a highly skilled tailor who had a close encounter with the Devil.

Understandably the tailor went home very frightened. Next morning his wife got up ready to scold him for drinking away their profits yet again, but instead found her husband stone-cold sober and cowering in the shop. He had a bolt of his finest woollen twill out and his shears ready to cut, but he was trembling so badly that he could not even start. His wife soon got the story out of him and she sent him off to see the local vicar, a man famously skilled in dealing with the forces of evil.

When the tailor came home that afternoon he had a smile on his face. He set to work on the Devil's coat. Seven days later it was finished. The tailor took the new coat out to the green at midnight and waited. Sure enough he soon saw the tall, striking figure of the stranger appear from the woods. The man came up and enquired gently after his new coat. The tailor produced it and slipped it on to the stranger.

'Ah', came the soft voice of menace. 'See here. The sleeve is too long.'

'So it is,' replied the tailor. 'I had not turned the cuff. Here, see how this button fixes it back.' The stranger nodded and studied the coat again.

'Ah', he said. 'See here. The lining is stitched loosely.'

'So it is,' said the tailor. 'I left it loose to allow the cloth to move easily. Here, pull this thread and see how it fits snugly.' The stranger nodded and studied the coat again.

'Ah,' he said. 'See here. This pocket is small.'

'So it is,' said the tailor. 'I made it small to hold the gloves I see you wear. Try this other pocket that I made deep enough to hold a brace of pheasants.'

And so it went on. For every fault the stranger found, the tailor had an answer. The vicar had advised him to build in a series of faults that could easily be rectified. Eventually the stranger gave up and glared at the tailor.

'You would seem to be as good a tailor as you boasted,' he said in his soft, menacing voice. 'Take your payment and go.' With that the man strode off and disappeared into the darkness.

The tailor went home, and he never drank again. Within a few years he was widely recognised as the finest tailor in northern England and gentlemen of fashion were beating a path to his door.

The tale is a good one but is probably too neat to be true. The idea that the Devil wanders the earth in the guise of a well-dressed gentleman features in many stories and tales, while the ending with its protagonist forsaking alcohol is another common theme. On the other hand, there is nothing to say that the Devil does not walk this earth. Judging by some events, he has had plenty of work to do.

CHAPTER 2

MYSTERIOUS LITTLE PEOPLE

Northumberland has long been a favourite haunt of the little people. These diminutive folk crop up in many guises and many places but always their magical powers make them instantly recognisable. There have been several attempts to try to solve the mystery of the little people, but the starting point must be to look at the creatures themselves, how they behave and what they look like.

Of all the assorted fairy folk of Northumberland none is so bizarre, peculiar or dangerous as the Hedley Kow. The village of Hedley on the Hill lies south-west of Newcastle, almost on the Durham border, but the Kow roamed the countryside all around there and were not confined just to the village. The Kow were first mentioned in writing on 7 August 1729 but were clearly widely known at that date and have remained so to this day.

The incident of 1729 was recorded only because an unfortunate servant named Thomas Stevenson, of Framwellgate in Durham, explained that he had been tardy in his duties because he had met the Hedley Kow. Obviously Stevenson thought that this was reason enough to be late, however, his employer did not accept things so easily and dragged Stevenson off to the home of Mr Justice Burdus and forced him to swear on oath that the events had taken place – which is how they came to be written down.

According to the affadavit, 'Thomas Stevenson, of Framwellgate in Durham, on 7 Aug., 1729, between eight and nine at night was returning from Hedley in Northumberland when he saw an apparition that looked sometimes in the shape of a foal, sometimes of a man, which took the bridle from off his horse and beat him till he was sore, and misled him on foot three miles to Coalburne. And that a guide he had with him was beat in the same manner, and that it vanished not until daybreak. His horse he found where he first saw the apparition by the Green Bank top, and said it was commonly reported by the neighbourhood that a spirit called the Hedley Kow did haunt that place.'

Since then the mischievous Kow has played its tricks on the unwitting folk around Hedley on numerous occasions. Each time it played a prank it adopted a different disguise, only revealing itself by its braying laugh when the unfortunate human victim had been run ragged.

In the 1870s an elderly woman was out collecting firewood, plucking sticks and twigs from the hedgerows around her home. She spotted a bundle of straw lying in the road and presumed that it must have fallen off some passing cart. Blessing her good luck, the woman picked up the bundle and slung it over her shoulder to carry it home. After a few yards she realised that the bundle was rather heavier than she had thought it would be but carried on regardless. Halfway home the bundle had grown so heavy that the woman was forced to put it down and have a rest. Thinking that perhaps the bundle contained something heavy, straw was at that date used as a packing material when sending objects any distance by horse and cart, she had a rummage through the bundle but it contained only straw.

Hoisting the bundle back on to her shoulders, she set off again but had gone barely a hundred yards before the crushing weight on her shoulders caused her to stumble and fall. The straw fell from her and rolled away. Cursing it, the old lady decided to leave it and return to collecting sticks. At that point the bundle of straw suddenly leapt upright of its own accord and began to dance a little jig in the middle of the road. Then the astonished woman heard the loud, jeering laugh of the Hedley Kow and realised that she had been tricked. The straw then flew off out of sight.

In 1889 a Hedley farmer named Forster, who should have known better, prepared to set off for market at dawn one summer's day. He had barely opened the stable door when his old grey mare came out to him, nuzzling gently at his hand. Forster had loaded his cart the evening before and was glad his mare was being so cooperative. He harnessed her into the shafts and set off trotting up the lane from his farm.

Forster had not gone far when his mare shied suddenly as if it had spotted something. Forster peered through the dawn gloom but could see nothing. He slapped the reins to get the mare moving again. After a few more yards the mare shied again. This time it occurred to Forster that the Kow might be about and up to its old tricks. He carefully backed the cart up until he could turn it around and then set off at a brisk pace to take a different route to market. He had gone barely a mile before the mare stopped again.

Determined this time to get through, Forster climbed down from the cart and warily moved forward to take his mare by the bridle and lead it forwards to face whatever prank the Kow had ready. Cautiously he advanced, soothing the skittish horse as he did so. Suddenly the mare reared up in alarm with a terrified snort and whinny. The farmer was sent flying. Forster scrambled back to his feet and began trying to calm the mare, which by now was bucking and kicking like a beast possessed. It smashed the cart shafts, tore loose the traces and careered around the lane. Forster looked around for the Kow, and then heard its harsh, braying laugh coming from the mare itself. The horse was the Kow in disguise. Disgusted, Forster trudged off home to find his grey mare waiting in the stable where it had been all along. He missed his day at market.

In the 1880s two young men set off from Hedley to meet their sweethearts who worked in a dairy nearby. The youngsters had arranged to meet at a road junction on the way to Prudhoe. When the two lads were still half a mile from the meeting point they saw their two girlfriends waiting for them and hurried on. The girls, however, moved off instead of waiting. The young men called out but were ignored, so began walking faster. The girls walked faster. The boys broke into a trot, the girls began trotting. The girls then moved off the lane and began walking at great speed over a field. The boys gave chase but were still unable to catch up with them. Suddenly they found themselves knee-deep in a muddy morass of bog and marsh. The two girls then turned around and came back towards the trapped boys. As they approached the 'girls' merged together into one horse-shaped beast that burst out laughing before vanishing. The Kow had struck again.

On occasion it was women who could get the worse of the Kow's sense of humour. On a spring day early in the 1870s a dairymaid went out to drive the cows in for milking. She had herded all but one of the cows to up by the gate and then turned back to encourage the final beast forward. The cow stood placidly munching on the grass until the girl was within a few feet, then it trotted off several yards and resumed eating. When the girl again approached, the cow again trotted off only to resume grazing. Time after time this happened with the girl and her quarry slowly moving away from the milking shed while the cattle that was already gathered together scattered back over the field. Eventually the girl lost her temper and stamped her foot before giving up and turning her back. Only then did the 'cow' start laughing with that peculiar 'har, har, har' of the Hedley Kow.

The Hedley Kow could cause trouble even when it was not actually present. One evening in the 1840s John Brown of High Field Farm was riding home when he saw ahead of him another man on horseback. Thinking it would be more pleasant to ride in company than alone, Brown put his horse into a trot. The man in front was another local farmer. Hearing the hoofbeats from behind him, he glanced round and saw a mounted man approaching at a trot. At once he thought the newcomer might be the Hedley Kow about to play some sort of prank and put his spurs to his own horse to force it into a trot.

Brown saw the man put on speed and so urged his mount into a canter. The other farmer, now convinced that he had the Kow on his track, likewise broke into a canter. The pair had covered over a mile at this speed when it suddenly occurred to Brown that he was chasing the Kow.

'Stop, Stop,' he called out. 'If thou be man.'

The other farmer drew rein and shouted back, 'In the name of the Father, the Son and of the Holy Ghost, what are thou?'

'Why I'm Johnnie Brown of High Field,' came the reply. 'Who's thou?'

Once the two men had assured themselves that the other was who they said they were, they had a good laugh at the incident.

However, the Hedley Kow was not always a subject for mirth. The local historian Stephen Oliver recorded one incident when the Hedley Kow was lurking outside a farmhouse one night, hooting, shouting and generally stopping everyone from sleeping.

The hills above Hazelrigg are home to the Hazelrigg Dunnie, a most mischievous entity.

The farmer grabbed a stout cudgel and went outside to drive away whoever was making the noise. No sooner had he stepped over the threshold than the cudgel was snatched away by unseen hands. The weapon then proceeded to batter the farmer senseless until he lay unconscious in a bloody pool in the farmyard. The Kow hooted with derisive laughter and fled.

Even less pleasant was the Kow's trick played upon the husband of a pregnant woman. When the woman went into labour the man rode off to fetch the local midwife. He found the woman at home, lifted her up to sit behind him on his horse and set off home. They had got only halfway there when the Kow appeared and caused the horse to bolt, throwing man and midwife into the hedge. By the time they got to their feet the horse, and the Kow, had gone. Forced to continue their journey on foot the pair arrived at the house to find the pregnant woman both frightened and in some distress. Fortunately all ended well for both mother and baby – but no thanks to the heartless Hedley Kow.

Rather similar to the Hedley Kow, but less well known and less active, was the Hazelrigg Dunnie which lived around Belford Moor and the hills of Cockenheugh toward the north of the county. This fairy beast took the form of a dun-coloured foal or pony which would pretend to be docile and gentle to tempt the unwary into trying to capture it, or even to mount it. It would then revert to its true violent nature to throw the human to the ground. It was said to have a particular liking for pregnant women, a clear link to at least one story about the Hedley Kow, so unknown horses were often kept away from women who were close to childbirth.

Both of these fairy beasts belong to a class of beings that folklorists classify as 'bogey beasts'. These entities share many features in common. They can change their shape at will in order to hoodwink their human victims, they delight in causing mischief and they never speak. The precise origin of these enigmatic beings is unclear, but most researchers link them to the fairy folk. Interestingly they are more common the further one goes in the north and east of England, so it comes as no surprise that Northumberland has two such entities which are firmly believed to exist.

Equally insensitive to the troubles it caused was the sprite that took up residence in Lark Hall, just outside Alwinton. In 1800 this grand farmhouse was the home of Mr Turnbull, a wealthy butcher from Rothbury. One day as the Turnbull family sat at lunch there came a strange series of knocking noises from inside one of the walls of the house. Thinking that maybe a rat or similar animal had got stuck, the family ignored the noises which stopped after an hour or so. A few days later the knocks returned, but this time with more violence. The bangs and thumps sounded as if a man with a hammer was pounding on the walls and doors, but nobody was there. These noises continued, off and on, for several days.

Things then took a more dramatic turn. Plates and cups stored on the sideboard in the dining room began moving by themselves. They would dance along the sideboard shelves in short skips and more than one would tumble down to smash on the flagged floor beneath. When the table and chairs in the same room began to jump and spin around, Mr Turnbull decided that he had had enough. He sent for the Reverend Lauder of Harbottle who was reckoned to have some skills in such matters.

A few days later the Revd Lauder arrived. He had taken only two steps into the house and was still in the process of greeting Mr and Mrs Turnbull when the family Bible was lifted by invisible hands from the window sill where it had been resting. The book flew around the room twice then hurtled straight toward the alarmed clergyman's head. The Bible stopped before making contact and then floated gently down to come to rest at the Revd Lauder's feet. Despite this rather disconcerting beginning, the vicar's visit seemed to go well. After he had left the sprite was quiet for a few days, but it was soon back to its old tricks.

Next Mr Turnbull invited in a pair of local wise men to see if they could achieve anything. The first wise man took one look at the house and left, declaring that whatever was to blame for the trouble was beyond his powers to drive away. The second did his best, but fared no better. In desperation Mr Turnbull put an advert in the Newcastle press offering 20 golden guineas to anyone who could clear his home of the invisible sprite. There were no takers, but the Turnbulls need not have worried. The invisible sprite left of its own accord some six months after it had arrived.

A very similar sort of entity to this is the Craster ghost. This invisible spirit inhabits the old tower that guards the road just inland from Craster fishing harbour. These days Craster is most famous for its kippers — and very tasty they are too — but the present secure harbour dates back to only 1906 when it was built to honour the memory of a son of the Craster family who had died fighting during the British invasion of Tibet. Before that date the fishing boats had to be pulled up on to the beach, sheltered only by the headlands on either side.

The village was formerly best known as the birthplace of Duns Scotus who was born here in 1265. Scotus became a Franciscan monk at a young age and soon gained a reputation as a brilliant scholar, philosopher and theologian. He was nicknamed 'The Subtle Doctor' as he travelled around the great universities of mediaeval Europe before he died in Cologne in 1308. In the 16th century his followers gained a reputation for their obstinate refusal to accept new ideas, giving rise to the word 'dunce'.

When Scotus was born here the Craster Tower and the land for miles around had been in the hands of the Craster family for around 70 years. Before then it had been the site of an English farmstead and before that a Roman fort. The tower seen today is the result of a Victorian renovation of what is a 15th-century construction, though parts of the central tower date back to the 12th century.

The old castle at Craster is home to an invisible spirit which manifests itself just before a member of the Craster family dies.

What has remained constant through all the building, demolitions and rebuilding has been the presence of the Craster ghost. Most of the time the phantom remains unseen and quiet. However, every few years it will become every bit as active and troublesome as the Lark Hall sprite. Furniture will be moved by unseen hands, pots and pans will crash about the kitchen and loud bangs or knocks sound out from the walls and doors. What makes these disturbances all the more upsetting is that they are traditionally said to be at their worst just before a member of the Craster family dies.

The spreading Craster estate was broken up and sold off piecemeal during the 20th century. However, the Craster Tower remains in the hands of the family, who must be awaiting the next visitation of the ghost with some trepidation.

The behaviour of the Lark Hall sprite and, to some extent, the Craster ghost fit almost precisely into a class of little people that are known across northern England as boggles or boggarts. These fairies are said to be invisible, mischievous entities that take up residence in a house for a time for no known reason. They will wreak havoc while they are present. On a very few occasions they will communicate with their victims either by writing notes or by using their ability to rap or knock to answer questions posed to them. It is usually said that it is a good idea to treat the boggles with great respect, for if they are mocked or ignored they will go on to cause even greater damage than before.

In more recent years researchers have labelled these sorts of hauntings as the work of 'poltergeists', a German term. These visitations almost invariably begin with bangs or knocks on walls and furniture before moving on to rather more disturbing events such as dancing furniture, smashed crockery and objects that float about the room. More extreme cases have stones thrown at windows, sudden deluges of water from nowhere and even fires being started in bins of waste paper or stacks of neatly folded laundry. Fortunately these hauntings tend to fade away after a few months, though they can be extremely disturbing while they last.

Exactly what causes a poltergeist attack is not clear. Researchers have shown that most poltergeist events take place in a house – rarely a workplace – where an adolescent is living. Very often, but not always, the youngster is undergoing emotional strain of some kind, typically an unhappy love affair, important examinations or attending a new school. Some believe that the events are caused by an outside spirit or entity which latches on to the emotional youngster to break into our world from its own. Others think that the youngsters themselves are inadvertently causing the bizarre happenings by some paranormal form of mind power that is not yet fully understood.

Such creatures as Hazelrigg Dunnie, the Hedley Kow or the Craster ghost may be mischievous or unpleasant to encounter, but they are as nothing compared to the terrible being that lives at Black Heddon and goes by the rather innocuous name of Silky. She is

The Blackheddon Burn is the home to the ominous and sometimes bloodthirsty fairy known as Silky of Black Heddon.

The prosaic concrete bridge which replaced the old stone bridge where Silky of Black Heddon used to sit, causing car crashes as easily as she had earlier overturned farm carts.

said to have been given her name because she was always dressed in a long dress of the finest black silk. All the known versions of the tale of Silky of Black Heddon indicate that the woman in question was a real person who lived many years ago, though when is never clearly stated, but who now survives as an incarnate spirit of some kind. The earliest reference to her comes in the 1770s but belief in Silky was widespread even then.

This Silky was a beautiful but malevolent woman who lived close to the Blackheddon Burn that runs south of Black Heddon. She had numerous strange habits, which she indulged in to the great annoyance of the local humans. She loved to jump up behind riders as they passed by, causing the horse to bolt at high speed while she clung on to the rider and shrieked with delight. The breakneck ride would continue for miles until the horse collapsed in exhaustion.

On other occasions, Silky would bring horses to a sudden stop. One day a carter from Black Heddon went to Newcastle to buy a load of coals to sell in the village. The return journey went well until he reached the narrow stone bridge over the burn south of the village. There he encountered Silky, who held up her hand to stop the horses. Once the horses had come to a halt, she slipped over the parapet and vanished. The alarmed carter waited for a while but when Silky did not reappear he decided to resume his journey. However, no matter how gently the carter coaxed the horses, nor how diligently he plied his whip, the horses would not move and the cart remained stuck where it was.

After an hour or more a man happened to come by. When he heard the cause of the trouble the man fished out of his pocket a piece of rowan wood that he had been whittling. Once the horses and harness had been stroked with the rowan, the spell was broken and the horses would move again.

Silky was sometimes seen flitting about the banks of her burn as if looking for somebody to tempt into the waters to join her. Some said that she was lonely and craved human company, others that she sought to lure men to their death by drowning. She certainly had something of the touch of death about her. In 1861 an elderly widow named Mrs Pearson was visited at home by the local vicar, the Revd J.F. Bigge. The clergyman asked the old lady how her health was. She replied that she felt well enough, considering her age, but that she knew that she would die very soon because Silky had come to sit on her bed the night before. The Revd Bigge tried to reassure the woman, but she was quite calm and matter of fact about the visitation. Three days later she died of a sudden stroke.

Certainly Silky's bridge acquired an evil reputation. During the 20th century the bridge was among the most dangerous accident black spots in Northumberland. Many cars skidded off the road at the sharp bend to its south, or collided with another vehicle coming the other way. Eventually the ancient structure was removed and replaced by a wide, concrete structure.

The number of motoring accidents at the bridge has lessened since the work was carried out. Some folk say that Silky has left the Blackheddon Burn forever. According to one version of her story, Silky was the spirit of a woman who had lived at Black Heddon many years ago, but who had died without telling her heirs where her considerable fortune was hidden. It was this omission that preyed on her mind and forced her to remain earthbound. Some time in the 19th century the ceiling of an old farmhouse kitchen fell in, bringing down with it the skin of an old black dog in which were sewn a large quantity of golden guineas. Thereafter, Silky was seen no more.

Silky has not gone away. Her baleful influence over the car crashes at her bridge testifies to that, so do the ominous stories of her determination to claim a life for her stream at regular intervals. In any case, Silky's behaviour simply does not fit that of a ghost – no matter how disturbed. Her origins must be sought elsewhere.

Silky causes accidents, summons the dead and plays dangerous tricks on humans. These traits, along with her beauty, link her to the pagan goddesses of the Celts. These female deities were said to inhabit the borders between water and land and to have a particular affinity with fords and bridges. They could be terrible harbingers of doom, but could also be well-disposed toward humans. Each stream or river had its own patron goddess, several of whom were worshipped with human sacrifice – a fact that may find an echo in Silky's attachment to death.

Perhaps Silky was, in origin, one of the many goddesses worshipped by the local Celts before the arrival of the English. If so, she has done remarkably well to survive so long. She may have descended in importance from a goddess to whom people were sacrificed, to a girl in a silk dress who is blamed for car crashes, but she is still around. After 2,000 years that is good going.

A rather different explanation may lie behind the enigmatic little person known as Bluecap who lived in Shilbottle Colliery during the 18th century. Bluecap was helpful, friendly and always welcome. He was said to live underground in the coal mine, where he survived for many decades before he apparently left in the 1840s. He was said to love working as a putter, that is as one who hauled the small trucks laden with coal from the coal face to the foot of the shaft where the coal was put into tubs to be pulled up to the surface.

Tradition states that, for many years, Bluecap demanded and received the wages of a human putter. The mine foreman would carry Bluecap's wages down into the pit and leave them on a rock in an isolated and little frequented corner of the mine. If the wages were

Shilbottle Colliery has long since gone and little marks its passing except for the sign to Colliery Farm. The underground workings were home to the fairy Bluecap, who may still be down there for all we know.

short he would leave them where they were in disgust, but if he were overpaid he would take only what was his due and leave the rest. This interest in money is a very unusual trait among the little people, who are generally contemptuous of human things.

Several miners claimed to have seen Bluecap about his work, and it is interesting how they described him. He was said to take the form of 'a light blue flame flickering through the air that would settle on a full coal truck'. Accounts then differ as to what happened next. Some said that the coal truck would move off of its own accord. Others that it instantly became as light as a feather so that the human putter could shift the heavy load with one finger.

The description is interesting for various reasons. The more helpful fairies are usually described as being either invisible or preferring to carry out their work at night when they would not encounter humans. For Bluecap to be seen quite so often by the miners makes him almost unique among such sprites.

Some have speculated that Bluecap was simply an explanation for some natural phenomenon that occurred down the Shilbottle Colliery. Something caused a small blue flame to flit about on the hewn coal, and was explained by the miners as being the little blue bonnet of a fairy named Bluecap. However, flames of any kind down a coal mine are exceptionally dangerous. The invisible explosive gas known as firedamp is contained in coal-bearing rocks and may seep out into the mine without warning. If it comes into contact with a flame, an explosion with fatal results is likely. Similarly, the finer grades of coal dust may float in the air and will likewise explode if they meet a naked flame. Thousands of miners around the world have been killed by such underground blasts.

Yet the miners of Shilbottle were quite unperturbed by the little blue flame that they saw dancing about the mine. They seem to have recognised that it was not dangerous and instead regarded it with favour.

Another of the little people who live in Northumberland is Hobthrush. Unlike Bluecap, Hazelrigg Dunnie or the Hedley Kow, Hobthrush likes to wander about the county and has several places where he may linger.

Accounts differ, but it seems that he first came to Northumberland in the 16th century when he is recorded as arriving in Elsdon. There lived in Elsdon at the time a middle-aged couple whose children had left home and gone to seek their fortunes elsewhere. This left the farmer with too much land to look after properly and his wife with too many chores to do. No matter what the season of the year, she could never get all her work done on time. The house suffered as the floors went unswept, the brass candlesticks unpolished and the cutlery poorly cleaned. There was never enough money to afford hired help, and things were only ever put straight when one of the children came home for a few days.

The village of Elsdon, seen from the hills to the south. It was here that the famous Hobthrush lived when he first came to Northumberland.

Again and again the woman complained, saying how much she hoped for somebody to help her. One summer's morning she came downstairs to find everything was perfect. The cutlery was cleaned and put away, the brass candlesticks were polished until they shone and the floors were not only swept but washed as well. There was not a speck of dust or dirt anywhere. The couple were amazed, but assumed that some kind neighbour had come in overnight to do the work. They speculated whom of the good folk of Elsdon had helped them out, but could not guess.

The next night the same thing happened: the house was tidied and cleaned to perfection by some mysterious intruder. After a week or so of this, she decided that she had to do something for her unknown helper, so she left out a dish of sliced bread and butter and some of the elderberry wine for which she was famous. Next morning the work was done as usual and both bread and wine had been consumed.

For months the arrangement went on quite happily. The housework was done every night by some mysterious intruder, while the grateful housewife left out food and drink each evening for her helper. The couple were delighted, having at long last a bit of time to themselves. She loved to sit in her garden in the evening and listen to the birds, while he was grateful for the tidy home.

One evening in the autumn, the man of the house was called out to help a neighbour with a sick cow. It was well after midnight by the time he was returning home. As he approached his house, the man saw that a light was coming from the kitchen window. Eager to find out which of their neighbours was cleaning their house, the man crept silently up to the door and peered in through a crack. He was astonished to see that their helper was no human but one of the little people.

The diminutive fairy was about three feet tall and looked to be quite young. He had brown hair, ruddy cheeks and bright eyes, which gave the appearance of being in very good health. However, his clothes were all in tatters: his brown cap was tattered and torn; his green jacket was worn out at the elbows and frayed around the cuffs and collar; and his red trousers were patched and torn. The man knew enough about fairy folk to be wary. He retired to a safe distance and waited until he saw the fairy leave before he let himself in and went to bed.

The next morning the man was eager to tell his wife all about their fairy helper. They speculated as to how they had earned the gratitude of the little man but they could think of no reason why he had come to help them. After some fruitless talk, the woman declared 'Well, I cannot let the poor little man go cold and ragged. I will make him a new suit and a cap.' She got her husband to fix the intruder's height as precisely as he could by comparing the fairy to objects about the house and then she set to work to make up as perfect a set of little clothes as she could.

Two weeks later the outfit was complete. She had made a cap of fine red felt, a jacket of brown velvet and trousers of green worsted. She had stitched a fine pheasant's feather on to the hat and added a pair of socks for good measure. Then the clothes were laid out in the kitchen and the couple slipped upstairs. They did not go to sleep, but lay awake waiting for the fairy to arrive.

Around midnight they heard the latch of the front door lifting gently and the door open softly. They crept down the stairs to a dark corner from where they could see into the kitchen. They watched as the little man got out the cleaning brushes and mops. Then he caught sight of the new set of clothes laid out for him. He ran to the table and, quickly throwing away his tattered rags, slipped into his new clothes and stood admiring himself. Then he gave a little laugh that turned into a wail. He called out loudly:

'A new suit, a new hood!

Hobthrush will do no more good.'

With that the little man let himself out of the house, leaving the cleaning tools scattered around and having done no work at all. He never came back to that house at Elsdon, but he had not left Northumberland: far from it.

Exactly where Hobthrush went next is unclear. It is most likely that he took to wandering around the county. He certainly went out to the tiny, low-lying islets that lie beyond the Farne Islands off the coast at Bamburgh. There he was said to ride a goat along the beaches, prance about in the spray and would take great delight in storms that could spell doom to unwary sailors. Hobthrush would shriek with laughter or with fury – depending on which version of the tale you follow – whenever a ship passed by.

One day the priest who cared for the little chapel on Inner Farne found Hobthrush cavorting around the island. Thinking that it was not right that one of the little people should make sport on so holy a spot, the clergyman asked him to leave. Hobthrush merely laughed and taunted the man of God. Determined to have his way, the cleric pulled out a jar of holy water that he had brought with him. Spotting the water, Hobthrush gave a shriek and galloped off on his goat at high speed. The clergyman gave chase, but found himself unable to catch up.

Eventually, the cleric gave up trying to catch the little man and instead he decided to trick him through a series of nonsense tasks. First, he took a fishing rod, baited the hook and began casting it on to a rock instead of into the sea. While Hobthrush watched, the cleric took his stew pot, put the ingredients for his meal underneath it and lit a fire inside it. Hobthrush came closer to get a better view. Then the clergyman crouched down and began fiddling with something on the ground. Wondering what the man was up to now, Hobthrush came even closer. Suddenly, the man sprang up and flung the holy water over Hobthrush, instructing him to leave the holy ground of Inner Farne for ever.

Hobthrush screamed and fled over the water to his remote island home. The clergyman then erected a fence of straw on the shore of Inner Farne facing out toward Hobthrush's home, sprinkled it with holy water and painted a cross on it. Hobthrush never returned to Inner Farne.

The precipitous heights of Callaly Crags where Hobthrush grinds the corn he steals from the granaries of honest farmers.

He did, however, roam widely over Northumberland. One location where he can be guaranteed to be found in the early autumn of each year is up on the Callaly Crags, those rugged hills overlooking Callaly Castle east of Lorbottle. Tucked away in the hills is a deep cleft which contains a number of potholes, in which a number of heavy stones brought down by winter spates are trapped here when the waters fall in the summer. It is said that Hobthrush uses these stones and holes to grind his corn.

Where he grows the corn that he grinds at Callaly Crags is not clear. Some say he has a private field, others say that he steals grain from the granaries of farmers – honest and wicked – and uses this for his mills.

Elsewhere, Hobthrush has been routinely blamed for accidents and praised when work goes well. He seems to be a fairly ubiquitous member of the fairy race in the county.

There are, however, large numbers of other fairy folk in Northumberland. These troops of little people do not have specific names, but they are widespread nonetheless. One of their favourite places is Elsdon, so perhaps it was not so much of a surprise that Hobthrush chose this village as his first home in Northumberland.

Two or three centuries ago, Elsdon was home to a woman named Howdie. She was highly skilled in the use of herbs for medicinal purposes and was especially good with pregnant women and childbirth. Whenever any woman in the area neared her time, Howdie would be invited to drop by to ensure that everything went smoothly. She did not charge for her services, but was grateful for any pies, jars of jam or other treats that her patients gave to her.

One evening, there was a loud pounding on her door. When Howdie opened it, standing before her was a tall, handsome man dressed in expensive clothes, on which was embroidered a coat of arms that she did not recognise. The man explained that his lord had urgent need of her services to tend a woman in childbirth. He promised to pay well and handed over a purse of silver as a sign of goodwill. There was, the messenger said, a condition: Howdie would have to ride behind him blindfolded as the lord did not want her to know where she went or who she tended.

Howdie was broad-minded enough to know that not everyone led an entirely respectable life. She suspected that the lord, whose name was not mentioned, had got a girl pregnant and wanted the child born in secrecy so that the scandal could be hushed up: such things were not unknown. The young woman and her baby would be sent to stay with relatives some distance away and be paid a modest sum to maintain the child. She had heard of such things and so agreed to go.

To Howdie's surprise, however, her blindfolded ride did not last very long. When she dismounted from the great charger, she was led by the hand across what felt like a stone courtyard, up some steps and through a door, then across a room and through another door. Only then was she allowed to take off her blindfold. Howdie found herself in a cosy and pleasant room with a bright fire blazing in the grate. Lying in a large bed was a beautiful young lady in the throes of childbirth. An old woman rose from a chair and hurriedly explained to Howdie how far the labour had progressed and the problems that had been encountered. Howdie knew her business well and had brought her herbs with her. Before long, the woman was calmed and the problems solved. The child was born in the small hours of the morning and appeared to be a healthy baby boy.

The old woman then pushed a pot of ointment into Howdie's hand and told her to rub a small amount into each of the baby's eyes, but to be careful not to let the ointment touch her own. The old woman then went to talk to the new mother, leaving Howdie with the baby. Howdie began to dab the strange ointment into the baby's eyes, but at that moment she had an itch over her left eye and inadvertently rubbed it with the finger carrying the ointment.

Instantly, the scene in front of her changed dramatically. Her right eye still saw a fine chamber, while her left eye saw only a dank cave. Where her right eye saw a fine blaze in a fireplace, her left saw a spluttering heap of cinders in a rough circle of rocks. Where her right eye saw a baby, her left saw a misshapen infant. Where her right eye saw a beautiful young woman resting in a richly decorated four-poster bed, her left saw a short, ugly woman on a pile of leaves.

Howdie knew at once that she had been misled by the magical glamour of the fairies. She was seeing them as they wanted to be seen, not as they truly were. The ointment she was putting on the baby's eyes revealed the truth. Knowing that the little people could be dangerous when crossed, Howdie decided to behave as if nothing had happened.

Howdie carefully cuddled the baby, handing it over to the old woman when she returned. She was then ushered out of the room to meet the messenger, now revealed to be a goblin on a donkey. Howdie was again blindfolded and climbed up behind the goblin. They rode off through the growing light of dawn, and Howdie had never been so glad to get home as she was that chilly morning.

For some days she contemplated the bag of gold coins that the goblin had left with her as payment. At first she feared that the gold was fake and hesitated to spend it. However, even when she looked at the coins with the eye which had touched the ointment it still appeared to be real gold. Then she worried that if she used fairy gold she might somehow be cursed or incur the wrath of the little people. Finally, she reasoned that fair payment for a job done was no trickery. Convinced that she could spend the money without problem, Howdie set off for Newcastle.

As Howdie wandered through the town, she bought herself some much needed new clothes and various luxuries. Then she moved down to the market to purchase some food.

While there she saw a figure, that she took to be a child, sidle up to a stall furtively. The child then whipped out a knife and scraped a little butter from the stall when the stall holder was not looking. Howdie watched the figure carefully as it slipped through the crowds and then approached a second stall. Again the knife came out, this time carving a slice of cheese without being noticed.

'Hey you,' cried out Howdie, gripping the child by the shoulder. 'Thief, thief, come and face the market manager.'

The child then squirmed around and glared at Howdie. With her left eye Howdie could see that the 'child' was in fact an old fairy woman. Howdie stepped back in alarm and at once the fairy woman realised that she had been recognised for what she truly was.

'Which eye do you see me with?' she demanded. Without thinking, Howdie put her hand up to her left eye. The fairy woman sneered. 'Then take that,' she shrieked and threw some powder into Howdie's left eye. For the rest of her life poor Howdie was totally blind in her left eye.

Fairy ointment also caused trouble for a farmer and his wife who lived at Netherwitton, near Morpeth, in the 18th century. One day the farmer and his wife were approached by a fairy couple who had with them a newborn fairy baby. The fairy couple explained that they lived nearby, but the woman had been called away to care for her sister, who was sick. The fairy man had a horse herd to care for, so they asked if the human couple would look after their baby for a few weeks. The fairies explained that they had seen the humans raise their own children and knew them to be good parents. The little couple offered to pay well, so the farmer and his wife agreed and took in the fairy baby.

As she was saying goodbye, the fairy mother handed the woman a small pot of ointment. She asked that the ointment be rubbed into the baby's eyes each morning, but warned her not to let it touch her own eyes.

All went well for several days. The fairy baby proved to be calm and settled, eating the mashed up carrots and gruel that it was fed with delight and sleeping soundly. However, one day, when his wife was out, the farmer could not resist trying the ointment on his own eyes. As he dabbed the mix into his eye the farmer felt a slight tingle, but otherwise, nothing happened. The farmer shrugged and got on with his life.

A week later the farmer went to the market in Longhorsely on an errand. While he was there the farmer spotted the fairy father leading a horse toward the stalls where the horses for sale were kept.

'How now,' called out the farmer. 'It is good to see you this day. I can tell you that your bairn is prospering with my wife and all is well at the farm.'

The fairy father turned suddenly and gaped at the farmer. 'How did you recognise me?' he demanded. 'You should not know me with my glamour.' Then the fairy father nodded and glared. 'The ointment, you used the ointment. You fool!' He then blew a powder into the farmer's eyes before leaping on to the horse and galloping off.

Within minutes the farmer was blind. He stumbled his way through the market, but fortunately was found by some friends, who led him home. When the farmer got home he found that the fairy baby had been taken by its father. The unfortunate farmer never regained his sight.

A miller named Hodgson also had cause to regret his dealings with fairies. Hodgson's mill stood on a stream just south of Rothley in the early 19th century, and was home to an entire family of fairy folk as well as to Hodgson. The little people, like Hobthrush in his more peaceful moods, did the cleaning and in payment took some of the grain stored at the mill.

The only downside to the arrangement as far as Hodgson was concerned was that the little people were in the habit of cooking their porridge in the kiln where he dried the grain. When they stirred the fire too much in order to give greater heat to the porridge, the fairies caused the parching grain to burn and become worthless. Still, it did not happen often and was more of a nuisance than a problem.

Soon a second family of little people moved in. The miller's housework was still done, but twice as much grain went missing and the parching grain was burned twice as often. Miller Hodgson began to lose patience. One evening he saw his parching grain beginning to burn once again and he lost his temper. Grabbing a great clod of mud and grass, the miller tossed it into the fire with a terrific thump. The clod scattered fire, cinders and boiling hot porridge among the hungry fairies who had been waiting for their meal to cook.

'Burnt and scalded!' screamed an angry fairy voice. 'Burnt and scalded!'

Realising that he had gone too far, the miller turned to run. However, he did not move fast enough and one of the fairies caught up with him and grabbed his ankle. The miller collapsed in a dead faint. When he came to his leg was paralysed and he never regained the use of it.

An altogether more dangerous fairy place is to be found high up on the wild Cheviot Hills, miles from the nearest road and only able to be approached in good weather, if the walker is not willing to risk being stranded out at night. It is here that the great chasm which goes by the name of the Hen Hole is to be found. The great slash in the hillside plunges down more than 250 feet from the hilltop, with rock-strewn walls so steep that the sun never manages to strike the bottom of the cleft. During some years patches of the winter snow survive in the Hen Hole well past midsummer. A small stream, the Coledge

Burn, comes out of the Hen Hole. It has long had a bad reputation, but just how bad was not clear until one day in the mid-17th century.

Today, fox-hunting with hounds is banned by law, but for many generations it was the only way to keep the population of foxes down to manageable proportions. In remote areas, like the Cheviots, the foxes were hunted by local shepherds and farmers, whose livelihoods depended on the lambs and chickens that the foxes would kill, given half a chance. Fox-hunting here was no sport: it was a necessity.

There was one shepherd called Ninian who lived by Kirknewton and who had as a mount a sturdy little pony. The pony was actually a pack animal, which was best suited to carrying essentials up into the roadless hills from the lowlands, but when a fox-hunt was to take place, Ninian would saddle up his pony. Unfortunately for him, the pony was much slower than any other horse or pony in the Cheviots and Ninian came in for a fair amount of teasing.

'We will hunt a tortoise for you next time,' one hunter would say as Ninian came up long after the kill.

'There is to be a hunt tomorrow,' a neighbour would call to Ninian. 'You should saddle up and set off today.' The teasing was good-natured and Ninian was content, so long as the foxes that ate his lambs were killed and he could join in the parties that followed every hunt.

One February morning the locals gathered for the hunt. They set off from Kirknewton and soon startled a fox that headed straight for the highest of the Cheviots. Those with the fastest horses gave instant chase, while Ninian and the others followed on as best they could. The chase was long and hard as the fox led them higher and higher into the hills. Soon, Ninian had fallen so far behind that not only had he lost sight of the pack and the lead huntsmen, he had even lost sight of the plodders. He drew rein and looked about himself.

Ninian found that he was not far from the Hen Hole. He did at least know his way home from there, so he sadly turned his pony's head and began to head back down the hills. It was then that Ninian heard the baying of the hounds. Glancing up, he realised that the fox must have doubled back on itself and was now running hard for the lowlands. Urging his pony into a trot, Ninian headed back up toward where he could now see the half-dozen lead riders following the hounds toward the Hen Hole.

Ninian was coming up fast when he saw the hounds disappear over the lip of the Hen Hole. He knew that they must be plunging down the steep, boulder-strewn slope into the very depths of the chasm. He was, therefore, not surprised when he saw the riders come to a halt on the edge of the slope. He would not have ridden down the drop, but would have entered the Hen Hole from where the burn issued out.

Just then the most wonderful thing happened: the sound of a woman singing drifted out over the hillside. It was without a doubt the finest voice Ninian had ever heard. He realised that it was coming from within the Hen Hole. Drawn by an irresistible impulse to get closer to the magical sound, Ninian dug his spurs again and again into the flanks of his pony.

Ahead of him, Ninian could see the half-dozen riders who had halted on the edge of the slope. They could hear the singing as well for they were peering down into the Hen Hole, as if trying to identify the source of the magnificent music. First one, then another of the horsemen urged their mounts forward and disappeared from sight down the slope. Ninian was coming up fast, but from where he was he could not see where the riders were going.

The final rider sat on his horse for a moment or two, peering down into the Hen Hole. The music continued to pull Ninian on; the urge to find the woman who was singing was irresistible. Surely the woman capable of such beautiful singing must be a wonderful person. As Ninian watched, the final horseman slapped his reins and disappeared over the brink.

Ninian was approaching the edge of the Hen Hole when the singing abruptly stopped, and he was left alone on the bare hillside with nothing but the moan of the wind in the grass to keep him company. Without the pull of the singing to draw him on, Ninian shied back from the edge of the steep slope in front of him. He peered down into the Hen Hole to try to see what had become of the men he had see plunge down only seconds earlier. There was no sign of them, nor of the hounds that had gone down first.

The men, horses and hounds had followed the call of the fairy singer of Hen Hole and were never seen again. Perhaps it is as well that the Hen Hole is so far off the beaten track.

The little people of Northumberland are therefore very far from being the dainty, carefree fairies of modern children's stories. They can be capricious and potentially dangerous to deal with, however, they are not all bad. Those met by Howdie and the Netherwitton farmer did not start out to do harm, but to enjoy a fair exchange. It was only when they realised that the human had not performed as instructed that the little people turned malevolent.

Indeed, some deals could be done with the fairies that were beneficial to the humans involved. Just outside Wooler there is an ancient earthwork known as Kettle Camp inside of which is a spring of pure, fresh water. This spring is held to be beloved by the local fairies, who will not drink water from any other spring or well in the area. If a young maiden desires something, she should take a new pin, bend it in half and bring it to the fairy spring. As the pin is dropped into the water the girl should say her wish out loud for the fairies to hear. If the pin has been taken away by the next day, the fairies will make the wish come true.

During the reign of Queen Victoria, a ploughman was out in the fields near Humshaugh on the banks of the North Tyne when he had his own beneficial meeting with the little people. It was a fine day as the ploughman went to work, plodding his way from one end of the field and back again. The horses were docile and the ploughman was proud to see that his furrows were neat and straight.

As he finished one row next to a willow tree, the ploughman heard some strange knocking and sloshing noises, as if a farmwife was churning milk in her dairy. There was nothing and nobody to be seen, however, so the ploughman guessed that he was hearing the fairy folk at work. When he reached the willow tree again he heard a little voice cry out:

"Tis a bad day today. What shall I do? I have broken my churning staff."

'I can mend that if you wish,' called out the ploughman. He did not wait for an answer, for he knew that the little people were usually shy and preferred not to be noticed. Off he went again to plough his furrow the length of the field and back again.

On his return to the willow tree, the ploughman saw a small churn staff snapped clean in two and lying on the grass at the edge of the field. Pulling his team to a halt, the ploughman fished out some twine and pins that he had in his pockets and swiftly bound up the two parts of the broken staff.

A field at Humshaugh, where a ploughman had a beneficial encounter with the little people during the reign of Queen Victoria.

'There,' he said. 'That will hold for the day, but I'd get a new staff entirely if it were mine.' Again he did not wait for an answer, but set off behind his plough team once more to plod up the field and down again.

When he returned to the willow tree the mended churn staff was gone. In its place was a thick slice of bread spread with a generous helping of butter. The ploughman ate it for his lunch and found it to be the best bread and the tastiest butter that he had ever come across.

Another dark chasm that is much loved by the fairies is to be found where the Brink Burn flows into the River Coquet. It is said that the little people are so fond of this place that they have chosen it to be their graveyard. On the rare occasions that a Northumberland fairy dies, the little people form a funeral procession and carry their dead to Brinkburn to inter beside the Coquet.

In contrast, the little people like to live at Netherwitton. The story of the unfortunate farmer who was blinded by a fairy began at Netherwitton, but other humans who came across the fairies here fared rather better. Most such encounters lasted only a few minutes and ended when the fairies ran off or slipped through a door set into the ground.

During the reign of King George III, the sources state that one day a dairymaid was returning from the fields with a bucket of milk balanced on her head. As she came down the path, the girl saw a group of four fairies running across a field. Every now and then a fairy would stop and bend down, as if to look at the flowers or the grass, before running on to follow its fellows. The girl watched them until they ducked into a hedgerow and then carried on to the dairy. She told her work colleagues of her sighting, but nobody else had seen the little people out that day. As the girl unwound the weise – the pad of cloth that kept the bucket steady on the head – a four-leaved clover fell to the floor. All present agreed that the girl had seen the fairy folk because she had had the four-leaved clover about her person.

Chathill, to the north of Alnwick, is another place where the little people like to live. In the 19th century there was a large fairy ring in one of the fields near there. The little people loved to dance around it at night, singing and laughing. During the day it was possible for humans to dance or run around it, but never more than nine times. Anyone who tried to complete a ninth circuit in succession was bound to fall or trip.

Just outside Lilburn stands an enigmatic stone called the Hurl Stone. Nobody is entirely certain how long this great pillar of rock has been standing here. Some believe that it is a mediaeval cross, but there is no sign of any carving on it and no inscription, nor is it close to any recognised Christian site that might explain its presence; others think that it was a boundary stone, but what boundary it marked is entirely obscure; while others still think that it is an ancient religious megalith dating back to the same time as Stonehenge. Only one thing is really known about the Hurl Stone: that it is beloved by the fairies.

The Hurl Stone is a great upright stone that has stood on the lonely hills of Lilburn for centuries. It is the site of fairy dances on moonlit nights when the little people chant their love for the stone.

On moonlit nights they will gather in the field where the Hurl Stone stands. While one fairy plays on a violin, the others will begin to dance. Round and round the Hurl Stone they will move, singing:

'Wind about and turn again,

And thrice around the Hurl Stone,

Wind about and turn again,

And thrice around the Hurl Stone.'

Again and again the simple words are repeated, while the tempo of the music quickens and the fairies are moving faster than the human eye can see.

The fairies were also said to feast and dance at Chesterholm, down among the ruins of the Roman fortress that historians now know was originally called Vindolanda. The Romans heated their homes in these chilly northern lands by means of a hypocaust system. The floors of their rooms were built two or three feet above the ground on a series of little pillars. A fire was then lit so that the smoke and hot air was drawn into the gap between the floor and the ground, thus heating the rooms above.

Since the Romans abandoned the site, however, the houses, barracks and other buildings fell into ruin. Very often little was left above ground other than the pillars and walls of the hypocaust system. To those who did not understand the system, these remains might have looked like miniature rooms and hallways for little people. Indeed, one 18th-century gentleman who came to view the Roman ruins was shown the hypocaust and assured in all seriousness that they were the remains of the ovens and kitchens of the fairies.

It may be that the presence of similar ruins at Housesteads (Vercovicium) led to that place also being labelled as a site for fairy feasts.

The fairies of Callaly also cluster around old ruins, though these are only a mere 500 years or so old. Again, as at Housesteads and Chesterholm, archaeologists have been able to uncover the truth behind the old stories.

There are various versions of what happened at Callaly, but the most usual tale goes as follows: Lord and Lady Callaly had decided to tour their estates in order to find a suitable spot on which to build a new castle. Lord Callaly chose a site high up on the hill, overlooking the village, stating that it was an easily defended spot in case the Scots came over the border and it also offered plenty of fresh air. Lady Callaly favoured a site down in the valley, which would be less windy and more comfortable. The two failed to reach an agreement, so in the end Lord Callaly took matters into his own hands. He summoned Master James, the finest castle builder in England, and told him to start work up on the hill.

Master James hired a gang of labourers, a team of stonemasons and a cook to feed them all, and began bringing in the stone, wooden scaffolding and everything else he would need. Having studied the site, Master James produced a design that would blend security from attack for Lord Callaly with a sheltered garden and warm rooms for Lady Callaly. The noble couple grudgingly accepted the compromise and Master James went to work.

After some weeks of toil, the foundations were laid and the stone walls could at last begin to rise. The stonemasons cut and shaped the blocks, while the labourers heaved them into position. At the end of the first day's labour, the first course of stones had been laid and Master James and his men marched happily down to the village for the night.

The next morning the builders climbed back up the hill to be greeted by a scene of desolation. The stones had been ripped up and scattered about and all their work was ruined. Thinking some prankster was at work, Master James set his men to work again. Once more they raised the first course by sunset, but when they came back the next day the stones were once again scattered and tumbled. A third time the work was done, but while the men marched down the hill, Master James hid in the heather to see what would transpire.

For hours Master James sat alone on the hillside. Finally, the last light in the valley was put out as the villagers and workmen went to bed. It was then that Master James heard a scampering and a rustling from high up on the hill. Down the hillside came a troop of fairies singing a little song:

'Callaly Castle built on a height,

Up in a day, down in a night.

Build it down in the Shepherd's Shaw,

It will stand for ever and never fall.'

Singing their song, the fairies tore up the stones and scattered them around until all the men's work was undone.

As soon as the fairies were gone, Master James went down the hill to report to Lord Callaly. The lord knew of a plot of land in the valley called the Shepherd's Shaw, so he wisely took the advice of the fairies and built his new castle there instead. As predicted, it stands to this day.

When archaeologists came to Callaly, they knew that the present castle was a 17th-century house built on to the side of a 13th-century pele tower. They had little interest in this structure, but had, instead, come to investigate the Iron Age hill fort that glowers down on the valley from high above and is generally said to be the site of the abortive castle building mentioned in the story. It came as a some surprise to them, but not to the locals, when the archaeologists found buried beneath the soil the foundations of a small stone

The dreaded Mab, the Queen of the fairies, lives upon Fawdon Hill above Otterburn. Seen here shrouded in autumn mists, the hill has long had an evil reputation.

castle that dated from the 13th century. The old tale was right; there had been an unfinished castle up on the hill after all.

Of all the fairy folk of Northumberland none was more powerful than Mab, the Queen of the fairies, who lived upon Fawdon Hill above Otterburn. It is said that the entire hill has been hollowed out to provide room for the royal feasting halls and palaces of Queen Mab. It is to Fawdon Hill that the little people come from all across Britain to pay homage to Queen Mab, to take part in her parties or to present their disputes for settlement. It is hardly surprising that so many fairy sightings have taken place on and around this hill, however, one in particular stands out.

Many centuries ago, a knight was riding over the moors toward Otterburn when he heard the sounds of music, laughter and happy chatter. Looking around, the man was amazed to see a great doorway opening into the hillside itself. Inside he could see a great hall in which sat a multitude of the little people enjoying a feast, while jugglers provided entertainment. Sitting on a great chair at one end was a beautiful lady dressed in the finest clothes the knight had ever seen.

The grand lady, no doubt it was Queen Mab, beckoned to the knight to enter and join them. As the knight hesitated, the lady waved a hand and a page came forward carrying in his hand a beautifully wrought silver goblet. The page handed it up to the knight. Just as the knight was about to drink the wine, he caught sight of a look of evil, gleeful triumph on the face of Queen Mab. Suddenly afraid, he tossed the goblet to the ground. Instantly, the fairy page vanished, the doors slammed shut and the knight was left alone on the hillside.

Anxiously, the knight waited to see what would happen next, but nothing did. He glanced down and saw that the fairy goblet was still on the turf. Taking a chance, he leapt down, grabbed the cup, remounted and galloped off. The knight, hoping to gain favour, presented the fairy goblet to King Henry I, who in turn gave it to King Alexander I of Scotland. The Scottish king does not seem to have believed in the goblet's fairy origins for he had it melted down.

Tales of the little people are to be found all across Britain. In many ways the Northumberland fairies, sprites and kows are not at all unusual. The ways in which they interact with humans echoes fairies from other counties and they are often linked to monuments that go back to prehistoric times.

Some researchers think that fairies and little people are simply creatures dreamed up by peasants in years gone by to explain things such as the Hurl Stone or the hypocausts of Vindolanda. Some believe that the fairies are the last remnant in human memory of the ancient race of people who lived here before the Celts and before the English arrived. Certainly, in some areas of Northumberland the fairies are referred to as pechs, which might be derived from 'Pict', a group of people known from Roman writings. Then again, sudden blindness or paralysis is traditionally blamed on fairies, when modern medicine would blame strokes or similar illness.

More recent research has pointed out the similarities between the documented behaviour of fairies and that of a quite different sort of little people, which is reported across Britain even today. Leaving aside the invented stories of fairy midwives, eye ointment and the like, the fairies of traditional belief can be shown to have some traits that link them. They live in isolated, rural areas where they have a great interest in the local flora and fauna. They resent human contact and will often flee or strike a human temporarily blind or immobile. Sometimes fairies will talk to humans, but not often. Above all there is no firm evidence that they actually exist, though those who have seen them are convinced. Turn now to the reports of the diminutive 'aliens', who are said to emerge from UFOs. These beings are about three feet tall, they are encountered only in remote rural areas and very often show a great interest in local flora or fauna. They will usually flee when they see a human, but sometimes they will cause the witness to be temporarily paralysed. The comparisons are close enough to suggest that modern 'aliens' and ancient 'fairies' might be identical beings, though what they really are is open to debate.

Whatever they are and however they might be explained, the little people of Northumberland remain a mystery. They are undeniably mischievous and tricky to deal with, and all things considered it is probably best to avoid them. So, if you are ever out near Fawdon Hill, or on the slopes above Callaly, and you see a diminutive figure some three feet tall, try to get away without being seen; doing so might save you a lot of trouble.

CHAPTER 3

MYSTERIOUS TREASURES

With border raiders and warfare a constant menace for centuries, it is no surprise that tales of buried treasure abound in Northumberland. It was common practice for farmers, drovers and even knights to convert much of their wealth to cold hard cash, and then to bury it in a secure place so that it would be safe if the Scots came over the border.

The vast majority of such stores of gold and silver were, of course, recovered by their owners. It was only if death intervened that the treasures were not retrieved. Local people would generally know if any farmer had such a stash of wealth, though not where it was hidden. If that person was killed in a raid or died suddenly it would be a common rumour that the location of the hoard was unknown. Usually the son or wife knew where the gold was to be found and quickly got their hands on it. However, that did not stop talk going around that a man could make himself rich if only he knew where to dig.

As is the way with legends, gossip and rumour, the size of the alleged lost treasure inevitably grows with time. What might have begun as talk about a farmer's secret hoard of a dozen gold sovereigns would grow in the telling until it was a huge chest bulging with gold and jewels of incalculable wealth.

One of the best known stories of a buried treasure is linked to Blenkinsopp Castle. This fortress was a key feature of the border defences, but after peace came between England and Scotland with the accession of King James of Scotland to the English throne in 1603 Blenkinsopp was no longer needed for defensive purposes. The structure passed through several hands, becoming little more than a rather grand farmhouse while the defences fell into decay. These ruins were, by the 1750s at least, said to be haunted by a lady dressed in a long white dress.

The story of the haunting was fairly widely known, but none of the written reports from this time contain any details other than the fact that the phantom was a lady. Then, in 1812, an event happened that revolutionised the story completely.

The rundown castle-cum-farmhouse came to be inhabited by the family of the manager, who was hired by the absentee landlord to look after the estates. One night the manager and his wife were awoken by the sounds of terrified screaming coming from the bedroom where their children slept. There they found their eldest son, who was about eight, sitting up in bed screaming, while the other children were looking around to see what was wrong.

The boy began to whimper out loud, 'The white lady. The white lady.' After a while he was calm enough to talk sense. He said that he had woken up a few minutes earlier to find a lady dressed all in white standing by the door to his room. He said the lady wore a long, expensive gown and jewellery. At first he had not been frightened, thinking that it was a local lady who had come to pay a visit to his parents.

The white lady had walked across the room and sat down on his bed. She had begun to wring her hands and to cry out loud. The boy had asked her what was wrong, whereupon the white lady had leant forward to kiss him on the cheek with lips as cold as ice. She had asked the boy to follow her, but the boy said he could not leave his younger siblings. The lady had then told him that if he came with her she would make him the richest man in Northumberland by showing him where she had hidden a chest of gold in the cellars of the castle.

Again the boy had refused to go with the lady. It was at this point that the mysterious intruder had become angry. She had demanded that the boy come with her and grabbed his wrist to drag him out of bed. The boy had wriggled free, whereupon the woman had bared her teeth in a snarl of rage and lunged forward as if to pick him up. That was when he had screamed out loud and brought his parents running: the white lady had vanished.

Blenkinsopp Castle was once a key fortress defending England from Scottish raiders, but is now a welcoming hotel. It is here that the terrifying white lady guards her hoard of gold and silver coins.

Unsurprisingly, the boy's parents put the tale down to a nightmare brought on by talk of their home being haunted. A few nights later, however, the white lady was back. This time the boy did not hesitate before calling out for his parents, but the lady vanished as soon as they arrived. After a third visit from the white lady, the children were moved to a new bedroom and the trouble did not reoccur.

Inevitably, news of the supernatural visitation, or nightmare, leaked out and soon everyone in the area was convinced that a vast treasure lay hidden in the cellars under Blenkinsopp Castle. A few people attempted a search but nothing was ever found.

In 1845 a writer producing articles on local folklore for a newspaper in Newcastle came to Blenkinsopp to investigate the story of the white lady. He found a few witnesses who had seen her flitting about the castle and surrounding area. Diligently, he managed to track down the boy who had spoken to the ghost — now a middle-aged businessman living in Canada. The two exchanged letters on the subject. The witness vehemently denied that he might have dreamed the episode and declared, 'I shudder still as if I can still feel her cold lips press my cheek and her wan arms stretching out in her death-like embrace.'

By 1895 the structure of Blenkinsopp was little more than a ruin and the then owner decided to stabilise the tumbling walls by propping up the foundations and re-pointing the stonework. While engaged on this task, the workmen came across a small doorway in the cellars that had been blocked up with stonework, which was now crumbling away. They at once jumped to the conclusion that this was the long sought for hiding place of the 'treasure of the white lady'. One man ran to get candles and a light, while the others tore down the stone wall blocking the doorway.

News spread and soon a sizeable crowd had gathered to watch the workmen investigate the opening. One of the workmen volunteered to pass through the doorway armed with a candle, promising to shout back to his fellows how he was getting on. The man proceeded gingerly, very sensible given the state of the crumbling stonework, and within a few yards found himself faced by a short flight of stone steps going down. At the foot of the steps the passage went on but it was now filled by an horrific stench. Bravely, the man went on until he found a second set of stone steps going down further. This second flight went down far beyond the reach of the light of the man's candle. He called back for advice from his workmates, who urged him to go on. A sudden gust of air belched up from the depths of the earth, extinguishing his candle and plunging him into darkness. He hurriedly blundered his way back to the first flight of steps, where he was met by another man with a fresh candle and together they exited the tunnel.

A quick conference was carried out among the workmen. They decided that the problem had probably been caused by the fact that the tunnel had been blocked up for centuries, allowing stale air and noxious gases to collect. They decided to wait a few hours to allow fresh air to circulate around the tunnel and then try again.

The second attempt, made by two men each armed with a candle, fared no better than the first. Again the first flight of steps were negotiated with ease and again the foul stench embraced the men. As they peered down the second flight of steps, another waft of bad air rushed up to engulf them and put out their candles. The men retreated hastily. This time the workmen decided that whatever lay down the tunnel was best left alone. They bricked up the doorway again and continued with their work.

It was about this time that the tale of Sir Bryan Blenkinsopp and his Moorish bride was recorded for the first time. It is not known whether this tale is a genuinely old story which explains the lost treasure of the white lady, or whether it was invented to provide a romantic backdrop to the events that had been occurring at Blenkinsopp Castle. The tale begins in the 12th century with Sir Bryan Blenkinsopp inheriting the castle and estates as a young man. The dashing young knight was considered a good marriage prospect by local families, but he declared that he would not marry unless he found a bride whose dowry was a chest of money so heavy that 10 men were needed to lift it. Whether Sir Bryan meant this, or if it were merely a ploy to put off the increasing numbers of suggestions that he was receiving, is not recorded. Certainly, Sir Bryan was enjoying being a single man, free of ties and responsibilities.

Sir Bryan then set off on crusade to fight against the Moslem hordes who were persecuting Christians in the Holy Land. The locals approved of their master's Christian devotion and bravery, but wondered if he would ever come home from such a dangerous adventure. They need not have worried. Not only did Sir Bryan come home, but he brought with him a Moorish bride, who had in her train a dowry chest so heavy that 10 men were required to lift it.

At first all went well for Sir Bryan and his exotic wife, but inevitably the new Lady Blenkinsopp came to hear about her husband's declaration that he would marry only a rich wife. She began to suspect that Sir Bryan had married her only for her money, not out of love for her. Relations between the two became frosty and then hostile. Eventually, Lady Blenkinsopp hid her dowry and refused to tell Sir Bryan what she had down with it. In a rage, Sir Bryan set off on crusade again. The months became years and no news came back to Blenkinsopp Castle. Clearly, Sir Bryan's rage was total and soon Lady Blenkinsopp repented of her actions. She sent letter after letter to the Holy Land, begging her husband to return, but no answer came. Eventually, news came that Sir Bryan had been killed fighting. Lady Blenkinsopp died of a broken heart within days.

Sir Bryan had left no will, so the Blenkinsopp estate passed to his brother. His inheritance was great on its own but he also wanted the Moorish treasure of the deceased

Thirlwall Castle was built using stones plundered from Hadrian's Wall. It soon became a refuge for the surrounding farmers whenever the Scots came over the hills to the north.

Lady Blenkinsopp. Despite his best efforts to search the castle and grounds, he never found it. To this day the treasure of the white lady remains hidden somewhere around Blenkinsopp. Perhaps one day somebody will follow her and become the richest man in Northumberland.

Another lost treasure complete with a supernatural guardian is that buried near Thirlwall Castle. This fortress takes its name from an old legend which states that after the Romans had left Britain, the Picts first broke through, or 'thirled', Hadrian's Wall, just north of here at Carvoran, and poured south down the valley of the Tipalt stream, on the banks of which Thirlwall Castle was built.

Be that as it may, the castle was constructed in around 1270 by the local Thirlwall family, who were charged with defending the valley from any marauding Scots who came over the border, just as the Picts had done so many years before. The Thirlwalls constructed their new castle using stones taken from the old Roman fortified barracks at Carvoran (situated on Hadrian's Wall) which was stripped down to ground level to provide dressed stone for the work.

The Thirlwalls flourished as a family and in around 1300 King Edward I stayed at Thirlwall Castle while inspecting the defences of his kingdom and preparing to attack the troublesome Scots. By 1440 the family had become so rich that the then Baron Thirlwall decided to impress his neighbours by making a table out of solid gold on which to serve

Thirlwall Castle is now a ruin, but in mediaeval times it was a comfortable home as well as being a secure base for the Thirlwall family, who built it in the 1270s.

from when they came to visit. The golden table of Thirlwall became a byword for ostentatious luxury across Northumberland.

Earlier Scottish raids had been beaten back by the Thirlwalls, but this time the Scots came in such force that Baron Thirlwall feared that his castle might be forced to capitulate. He summoned his jester, a dwarf of unsavoury reputation who dabbled in the dark arts of witchcraft, and asked him to take the golden table of Thirlwall to a place of safety.

'I shall take it where no mortal man may follow,' the dwarf replied. 'And I will not return it until you yourself come to claim it.' The dwarf then hoisted the table up onto his back and staggered out of Thirlwall Castle.

The next day the Scots arrived and laid siege to Thirlwall Castle. The fortress held out successfully, but an unlucky arrow shot from the attackers struck Baron Thirlwall and killed him. When the Scots retreated back over the border, the new Baron Thirlwall, son of the bold knight killed in the siege, began repairing the damage. Men were set to work rebuilding the houses and patching up the castle defences that had been damaged; messengers were sent south to tell the drovers and farming families that it was now safe for them to return with their livestock and equipment; and finally, a team of men were sent out to tell the dwarf jester to return with the golden table of Thirlwall.

The men assumed, like everyone else, that the dwarf would have carried the table off to one of the caves or potholes in the area, which he was small enough to climb into but which a full-grown man was too big to enter. They searched all the caves and potholes they knew of, calling down that the Scots had gone but they got no answer. Thinking that perhaps the dwarf suspected the calls to be a trick, the new Baron Thirlwall went himself to call out and assure the dwarf that the Scots really were gone. The dwarf, after all, knew the young man and his voice well.

Again there was no response. The new baron began to suspect that perhaps the dwarf had stolen the table and fled south to sell it. Riders were sent out to search the roads for a dwarf carrying a heavy load and to warn all goldsmiths that the table had been stolen. Nothing was found.

It was then that a farmer came forward with a bizarre story. He said that while he and his family had been packing up their goods ready to flee south to safety, the dwarf-jester had called to see them. The dwarf had, indeed, been carrying the golden table. The dwarf had asked the farmer to show him the farm's well, which the farmer had happily done. The dwarf had peered down the well, rubbed his chin and then muttered, 'This will do, this will do.' The farmer had paid no more attention, being busy getting his valuables packed on the cart and the livestock rounded-up for the journey south.

However, when he had returned to his farm, a most peculiar thing was to be found, or rather not to be found: the well had gone. It had not been smashed like the house and barn,

The dwarf of Thirlwall slipped out of one of the castle doors with the golden table of Thirlwall strapped to his back.

it simply was not there. Where there had once been a deep shaft in the ground, topped by a parapet and a winch for the bucket, there was now simply unbroken turf. The farmer had tried digging, but his spades and picks had broken.

Reasoning that the dwarf had hidden himself and the gold table in the farmer's well and then sealed the entrance with a spell, the new Baron Thirlwall set off to retrieve both. Arriving at the farm with a team of men, the baron began digging. As the farmer had said, however, the tools simply broke, as if the men were trying to dig through solid iron. The baron tried calling out to the dwarf, assuring him it was safe to emerge and that he really was the new baron.

It was then that the baron recalled the dwarf's final words: 'I will not return it until you yourself come to claim it'. However, the old baron to whom the promise had been made was dead, killed by the Scots. He could not come to claim the golden table of Thirlwall and so the dwarf's spell could not be broken. The magnificent solid gold table remains hidden in the enchanted well to this day, as does the dwarf of Thirlwall, who has not been seen since he sealed himself into the well. Nor is Nelly the Knocker, though for rather a different reason.

Nelly the Knocker was a ghostly lady who used to sit on a great slab of rock that lay in a field just north of Haltwhistle. The phantom took her name from the fact that she would sit on the boulder for hour after hour at night knocking at it gently with a small rock. For how long Nelly the Knocker had been knocking, nobody knew. She had been at it since before anyone could remember and the sound was a familiar one to the good folk of Haltwhistle.

Then, in around 1750, the farm on the land where the great stone stood was bought by an outsider from south of the Tyne. He was told all about Nelly the Knocker, but did not believe the stories until he himself saw and heard her. This farmer had two adult sons who became intrigued by Nelly and her knocking. Night after night, they would creep down to the field to watch the ghost at her work. After a while they began to speculate as to why the ghost spent so long on the apparently fruitless task of tapping a pebble against a boulder.

'Perhaps she is trying to break into the great rock,' said one son.

'Perhaps we should help her,' said the second.

The next day the sons persuaded their father to part with some money and went off to buy some gunpowder from a local quarry. They engaged a blaster to show them how to pack the powder and how to lay the fuse, and then returned to Nelly's rock. The young men packed the powder under the rock and laid the fuse. Glancing around to make sure that Nelly was nowhere in sight, they lit the fuse and took cover. The blast was enormous, shattering the rock to fragments.

The great treasure of Warkworth was stolen centuries ago, but the stone that marked its resting place has been built into the tower of the castle.

When the dust had settled, the two young men crept out to look over their handiwork. Where the stone had once stood there was now a gaping hole, in the bottom of which nestled a number of large clay pots. The first contained a mass of silver coins, the next an equal measure of gold coins. Each of the pots contained a small fortune, which together made up a vast treasure. The farmer and his sons were rich for life. However, Nelly the Knocker was neither seen nor heard ever again.

The belief that some ancient stones hide treasure is widespread across Britain. These upright stones, similar to those at Stonehenge and other famous monuments, date back to before 800 BC. They are generally believed by archaeologists to have been used for religious or ceremonial purposes, though nobody is quite certain. What makes the story of Nelly the Knocker unique is that the treasure was found and the mysterious stone destroyed. More usually the stories state that the treasure is still there and that disaster has struck anyone who has tried to unearth it. Perhaps there really was a treasure at Haltwhistle.

Another treasure that is said to have been recovered once lay beneath the Blue Stone of Warkworth. Some centuries ago the steward of Warkworth, who held the castle for the Percies, had a remarkably vivid dream. He saw a man wearing strange and unfamiliar clothes and carrying a heavy sack on his back walking along the banks of the river, but

The ruined castle at Dilston hides the vast treasure of the last earl of Derwentwater, but treasure seekers should beware for a demon is said to guard the hoard.

where Warkworth and its castle should have been there was nothing but open pasture land and scattered woods. The man came to an upright stone of a curious blueish hue, which the steward knew well. This man then proceeded to dig a hole beside the blue stone and poured a mass of silver and gold jewellery into the hole. He then covered it up again and the dream ended.

The steward decided that the very next day he would go to the blue stone, which stood only a couple of hundred yards away, and dig. He told his assistant to get a team of men prepared with shovels and ready to march to the blue stone. However, an urgent summons then arrived, demanding that the steward ride to Alnwick to see his master, Lord Percy of Alnwick. The steward rode off and did not return until the next day.

As he arrived in Warkworth, the steward was met by his men with the news that the assistant steward had not been seen all day. The man's rooms were empty and a horse and pack horse were missing from the stables. With a sinking feeling, the steward rode to the blue stone. Sure enough there was a large hole dug by the stone and a discarded shovel lay nearby.

Presumably, the assistant steward had followed his master's orders on his own account. He had found the treasure of the dream and fled with his new found wealth.

Not all supernatural guardians of treasure are as passive as Nelly the Knocker or as co-operative as the white lady. Dilston Castle was for centuries the home of the Radcliffe family, who rose to hold the title of Earl of Derwentwater. After the last earl was executed for treason in 1716, the estates passed to a remote cousin who chose not to live there, already having a comfortable house of his own. The castle was used as a farmhouse and barn until, in 1768, a fire reduced it to ruin.

It is under those ruins that the treasures of the Derwentwaters are said to lie. Local legend has it that the last earl buried his vast wealth before he set off to join the ill-fated Jacobite uprising which cost him his life. On that last night at his home, it is said, the earl summoned up a devil to guard his wealth until his return. The devil is said to squat on the sacks and chests of gold and silver in a chamber deep beneath the ruins.

Interestingly, the family that owned the Dilston estates before the Radcliffes was a Norman clan called the d'Eivills, the family tomb of which is in Hexham Abbey. Almost inevitably the name d'Eivill came to be pronounced 'devil'. Perhaps the story of a treasure guarded by a devil originally referred to a treasure hidden by the d'Eivills.

An equally dangerous guardian looks after the vast hoard of gold that lies beneath a small hill just outside Gunnarton. This treasure is guarded by a ferocious dragon that prowls the caverns and passages that lie underground here. Back in the 19th century one man bolder than the rest decided to explore the caves with the aid of a lantern. After all, he reasoned, dragons do not really exist.

The hill outside Gunnarton, where a vast stash of gold is said to be guarded by a ferocious dragon that prowls the caverns and passages which lie underground.

The man was doing well in his explorations. He had found no treasure, it was true, but then he had found no dragon either and was carefully keeping a map of the passages through which he crawled and walked. Then he found lying on the floor of a cavern the horribly mangled skeleton of a man. The body had clearly been there for many years. A short distance away lay another skeleton, again showing signs of horrific injury. When the man found a third skeleton in a similar condition, he decided that discretion was the better part of valour. He retraced his steps and was grateful to emerge back into the sunlight.

The tale of a dragon guarding a hoard of treasure is well-known from pagan English and Viking myths and legends. The best known of these is the epic English poem *Beowulf*, written around AD 800, in which the eponymous hero overcomes all sorts of monsters before finally being killed in combat with a dragon guarding a vast treasure hoard. Perhaps one of the caves in this region really did contain mutilated skeletons and the tale of the dragon might have been lifted from old legends and used to explain how the men had died.

Another treasure that is yet to be claimed lies in the waters of Cyper's Linn, a deep pool on the River Allan near Staward Peel. Quite how the treasure got there is not known, but it is said to consist of a great wooden chest containing gold. Many years ago, one local farmer decided to retrieve the treasure. He took his two plough horses, Brock and Bran, down to the river and attached to their harness a long chain that ended in a large iron hook. The farmer threw the hook into the river time and again until finally it caught on something.

Eager to get his loot to land, the farmer whipped the horses into motion. Slowly, inch by inch, the horses pulled and the eager farmer glanced back to see a weed-covered wooden chest emerging from the water. Applying the whip with greater enthusiasm, the farmer gleefully called out:

'Hup, Brock. Hup, Bran.

We'll have it out in spite of God or man.'

Perhaps it was his profanity, or perhaps it was the mere act of talking, but the words proved to be disastrous. There was a sudden flash of light and a loud rushing noise. At first slowly, but then with gathering speed, the treasure chest began to slide back under the water. To the farmer's horror, the chest dragged with it not only the iron hook and chain, but also the harness and the horses. Within a few seconds the farmer found himself alone on the river bank with nothing but a circle of bubbles to mark where he had lost his valuable ploughing team. It is said that when the river runs low in hot, dry summers the bodies of the horses can be seen resting on the bottom.

A treasure of a rather different kind lies beneath the waters of the River Coquet at Brinkburn. The monastery of the Augustinian canons at Brinkburn was founded in 1135 by Sir Bertram de Mitford and was subsequently richly endowed with lands by the Mitfords and other local families. Unfortunately, Scottish raids stripped the lands of much of their value, while the monastery was unlucky in having a succession of financially inept priors.

Eventually, the financial affairs of Brinkburn Priory were so bad that the house was put under the direction of the much larger and richer monastery at Durham. The Bishop of Durham offered to pay off all the debts of Brinkburn and to repair all the damage done by the Scottish raiders, but there was a condition. Brinkburn had the finest peel of bells in the North and the bishop wanted them for Durham. Sadly the monks of Brinkburn agreed. Workmen were brought in to lower the bells carefully to the ground and load them on to carts ready for the journey to Durham.

The road out of Brinkburn lay beside the Coquet. As the carts passed out of sight of the priory, the horses began to buck and caper about. Despite the best efforts of the carters, first one and then all the carts were overturned and the bells thrown into the river. Ropes and hooks were brought but nobody was ever able to extract the bells from the river.

As late as the 1890s, local children swimming in the Coquet would engage in the sport of 'diving for the Brinkburn Bells', confident in the knowledge that if the bells could be retrieved so would the lost treasure of the priory. The bells have never been located, still less hauled out, so the treasure remains hidden.

Yet another treasure lies beneath the waters of Broomley (or Broomlee) Lough, which is situated amid the wild moorland between Hexham and Hadrian's Wall. It is believed that in the 14th century a local lord was surprised by news of the Scots pouring over the border. Unable to stash his gold and silver coins in their usual place, the lord put them in a great wooden chest. He loaded this into a rowing boat and paddled out on to the waters

The bells of Brinkburn Priory are said to lie beneath the waters of the nearby River Coquet, complete with the accumulated treasures of the holy men of Brinkburn.

of Broomley Lough. Having reached a spot that he could be certain of finding again, the lord heaved the treasure chest over the side of the boat and watched as it sank beneath the dark, peaty waters of the lake.

The lord hurriedly pulled to the shore where he then came across a local wizard. The lord begged the wizard to put a curse on the treasure to ensure that nobody but he could ever retrieve it. The wizard lifted his arms and chanted:

'But let it lie till the crack of doom,

In the depths of the Lake of the Ley of Broom,

Unless some man of our kindly race

Should come to possess this pleasant place,

And let him then with two twin yauds,

Two twin oxen and two twin lads,

And a chain that's been forged by a smith of kind,

Get it out, if he can it find.'

The 'yauds' referred to are plough horses, while the 'smith of a kind' is a smith who is the seventh generation of his family to practise the trade. The mention of 'some man of our kindly race' is slightly obscure and the precise meaning of it is not quite clear. Some think that it means simply an Englishman, as opposed to a Scotsman – after all it was the Scots whose raiding caused the treasure to be dumped in the first place. Others, however, have pointed out that this is not much of a restriction, since most owners of land in Northumberland are English. Some folklorists have suggested that the rhyme refers not to an Englishman but to the lost race who held this land before the English arrived: the Celts. Thus, the restriction would make more sense and so would the events that followed.

A couple of centuries ago, it is said, the man who owned the land around Broomley Lough decided to retrieve the treasure of the lake for himself. He scoured the land until he found twin ploughing horses, twin draught oxen and twin boys to help him. Then he located a smith who was in the seventh generation of the trade and got him to forge a stout chain. Thus equipped, the man set off for Broomley Lough to make himself rich.

Arriving at the lough, the man sat down to watch the waters. He soon noted a spot where, whichever way the wind blew, the water surface remained unruffled by ripples. Reasoning that this must be where the treasure lay, the man hitched the horses and oxen to the chain and set off in a boat. He dropped the chain carefully on to the spot where he believed the treasure chest to lie, then he shouted to the twin boys to urge the horses and oxen to start pulling.

At first the chain rattled out of the lough easily enough, but then it snapped taut: the chain had caught around something heavy. The man rowed ashore and himself joined in urging the beasts to pull with all their might. Slowly, gradually, painfully, the animals made headway as the chain emerged link by link from the lough. Just as it seemed that the great treasure chest must be about to break the surface of the water, the chain snapped. Horses and oxen tumbled forward in a confused heap, which took the twin boys some time to untangle.

Greatly annoyed, the man waited until all was ready and then rowed out again to drop the chain. However, this time the chain did not catch on anything, and no matter how many times the chain was dropped, nothing was ever found. The landowner was, perhaps, not of 'our kindly race'.

Another treasure located on the windblown moors lies near Old Hazelrigg. This particular hoard is said to be the mass of gold and silver coins gathered together by a successful reiver, who plundered the Scots over the border. The treasure is said to be buried on the adjacent moors of Collier Heugh and Crocken Heugh, as well as at Bowden Doors, a pair of stone crags a few miles away at Lyham.

An old rhyme runs:

'In Collier Heugh there's gear eneugh

In Coken Heugh there's mair,

But I've lost the keys of Bowden Doors.

I'm ruined for ever mair.'

In 1880 a landslip occurred at Tynemouth. The collapse of the hillside below Tynemouth Castle brought to an end any attempts that might have been made to recover the lost treasure of Jingling Geordie, as it sealed up the entrance to the deep cavern known as Jingling Geordie's hole. According to legend, the vast hoard that lay in the depths of the cave was guarded by a pack of hell hounds, a tribe of goblins and a dragon.

Unsurprisingly perhaps, only one man is known to have tried to penetrate the deepest depths of the cave system to recover the treasure. This was Sir Walter the Bold, who after many adventures came home to Tyneside to settle down. As his last quest he entered Jingling Geordie's cave to try to find the treasure. When he emerged some hours later, it was with arms cradling a mass of gold coins, gold jewellery and silver tableware. Nothing, however, would induce him to go back in for more. He had, he said, barely escaped with his life from the horrors within and did not fancy giving the demonic creatures a second chance to take his soul.

That these tales of lost treasures and forgotten hoards of coins are not all folklore is proven by the events at Thorngrafton in August 1837. At that time the Newcastle to Carlisle railway line was being built and sleepers were needed. It was decided to reopen the Barcombe Quarry, just outside Thorngrafton, which had not been worked for generations.

It was later discovered that the stone for the nearby stretch of Hadrian's Wall had been excavated from here, which may have some bearing on what happened next.

A gang of workmen were stripping the heather and soil off a patch of ground so that it could be opened up to expose the rock beneath. One man, Thomas Pattison, found a deep cleft in the underlying rock and saw something glinting inside. He reached down and pulled out a bronze bucket shaped like a boat which had a bronze, semicircular handle. Nestling in the bucket were 63 Roman coins, all of them silver except for three that were of gold. The team of men were accustomed to pooling their wages to buy food and beer, so they decided to pool the coins. Thomas Pattison, who was rather better educated than the others, was sent off to Hexham to sell the coins so that the proceeds could be divided up.

Pattison hurried to see the town's solicitor. The solicitor told him that a similar but smaller collection of silver coins had recently sold for around £2, at that time a considerable sum of money. The solicitor offered Pattison £1 10/- for the coins, but Pattison refused. He then took the bucket of coins and gave them to his brother, William, who owned a farm at Blenkinsopp. Pattison then went back to the quarry to tell his workmates that the coins had fetched only a few shillings, which he then passed around.

Looking down toward Hazelrigg from the windblown moors of Collier Heugh. There is said to be a vast hoard of gold and silver coins hidden on these moors, gathered by a reiver who plundered the Scots over the border with great success.

A few weeks later, Pattison left the quarry to find a buyer for the coins. He approached a Mr Fairless, a local gentleman with an interest in Roman remains, who offered £10. Again Pattison refused the offer. However, news of the find reached the ears of the agents of Hugh Percy, Duke of Northumberland. In law, finds of gold and silver should be divided between finder and landowner, therefore the duke's agents sued Pattison for the duke's share of the value of the coins. Pattison went on the run and a warrant was issued for his arrest as a debtor. He was found some months later working in a slate quarry in Wales, while living with his cousin who was gamekeeper to Sir Watkin Wynn. Arrested for debt, Pattison refused to pay and was thrown into prison.

It transpired that Sir Watkin knew the duke very well and next time they met each other, in London six months later, he told the duke that he thought the treatment handed out to Pattison was harsh. The duke knew nothing about the matter, as it had been dealt with by his solicitor. He at once ordered the solicitor to withdraw the debt order and to instead come to some agreement with Pattison.

However, Pattison knew that a recently introduced law on bankruptcy meant that after serving 12 months in prison all his debts would be written off. He decided to stay put in the Welsh prison until the coins became his. Unfortunately, by the time Pattison was released and had travelled back to his brother's farm, his mind seems to have been affected. He refused to let anyone see the coins and took to wandering alone over the moors, even in the worst weather. He helped his brother out around the farm, but never again took a proper job. He died a few years later, apparently of 'melancholy'.

William Pattison then inherited the coins and put them up for sale. They were bought in 1858 by a Mr Clayton, who also owned the ruined Roman fortress of Chester and several miles of Hadrian's Wall. He in turn later passed them on to the British Museum.

If Northumberland holds more rumoured buried treasure than any other English county, it should not be thought that many are overly keen to find it. As shown by the sad story of Thomas Pattison, the finding of buried treasure does not always lead to happiness.

CHAPTER 4

MYSTERIOUS HISTORY

People have lived in Northumberland for as long as it has been possible for humans to survive here. Over the years they have left behind some of the most puzzling historic enigmas to exist anywhere in the world.

The very first mystery is to know quite when humans first came to Northumberland. The most recent ice age lasted from about 80,000 years ago until 15,000 years ago. The deep glaciers that formed had a great impact on the landscape of Northumberland, carving valleys, moving masses of rock and soil from one place to another: in short reshaping the county. All traces of humans who had lived here before the ice came has been destroyed. That humans lived here is almost certain. The famous 'Swanscombe Man' (actually a woman) from Kent died about 200,000 years ago and there is no reason why her relatives should not have got as far north as Northumberland. She belonged to a species of human known as *Homo erectus*. They had a body not very different from our own, but the brain was only about half the size of the modern average.

As the ice retreated from Northumberland some 15,000 years ago, humans moved in. The ice seems to have disappeared very quickly, possibly within the lifetime of a human, though more probably over a stretch of 300 years or so. By this date humans had fully evolved and now dominated Europe. For these people to get to Northumberland would not have posed much of a problem; they simply could have walked across what is now the North Sea.

At that date what is now the southern half of the North Sea was a wide, fertile plain. The Thames and the Rhine joined somewhere off the Danish coast to form a single great river that flowed north to enter the sea east of Aberdeen. The land teemed with game such as mammoths, wild cattle and deer. Undoubtedly, the first people to wander over this great plain to reach the low hills that are now the coast of Britain were hunters and gatherers, who lived off the bounty of nature, thriving in good times and starving in bad. As the ice glaciers further north melted, the sea waters rushed in to form first the North Sea and then, around 12,000 years ago, the English Channel and so cut Britain off from continental Europe.

The people living in Northumberland at this time belonged to a culture that archaeologists have dubbed Mesolithic, the middle Stone Age. This culture is characterised by a highly sophisticated tool kit composed of dozens of different types of tools made from bone, antler and stone. The people had not yet learnt farming in any form, though they may have been herding semi-wild animals as a convenient source of meat, hides and maybe even milk.

One of the more clearly defined cup and ring marks to be found on the great boulder of Roughting Linn. The mystery of why these elaborate marks were made has never been properly solved.

Exactly what these people looked like is not clear since so few of their skeletons have been found. For the same reason it is not yet known how closely they are related to modern Britons. There have been several movements of population both into and out of Britain since then, but it seems likely that at least some of our genes date back to these earliest Mesolithic settlers.

Farming came to Britain some time around 4,000 BC. It marked the transition from the Mesolithic, the middle Stone Age, to the Neolithic, the new Stone Age. It used to be thought that farming was brought in by a new race of humans, who drove the indigenous population virtually to extinction. That theory fell out of favour in the 1980s and was replaced by the idea that farming was a cultural import from the continent that was learnt by local people, and no real movement of population was involved. More recent studies have shown that the truth was much more complicated. While the mass of the population may not have moved, it is clear that there was a significant immigration, particularly among what are termed 'high status' individuals. Some experts believe these were a travelling community of craftsmen, priests or other trade specialists, who were respected and welcomed by the communities they visited. Others think it more likely the incomers were an invading warrior elite who imposed their rule on the locals. We simply do not know.

A similar sort of dispute exists around the so-called Beaker People, who began arriving in Britain around 2,000 BC and reached Northumberland around 200 years later. Some see them as peaceful travelling specialists, others as conquering warriors. Whatever the truth, these people were so named by modern archaeologists because their graves almost always included a small pottery bowl shaped rather like the beaker of a modern baby. They came from the Rhineland and brought with them stone working skills.

The marks of these people can be seen at several dozen sites across Northumberland, where they carved boulders and rocks, cliffs and crags with the mysterious 'cup and ring marks' that were a speciality of the northern Beaker culture. These enigmatic markings are found scattered across a wide band of territory that includes much of what is now northern England and southern Scotland, across to Ireland and down to north-western Spain. This indicates that these regions shared a culture that, while not identical across the great sweep of territory, was at least similar and distinct from that of northern Scotland and southern England.

The cup and ring markings are found mostly on natural boulders and rocky outcrops, though a few are carved into stones that have been set up by humans. It is difficult to date the markings, as grooves cut into stone contain little to help the archaeologist. It is usual to date the markings by their links to graves, burials and abandoned houses. Only a few of the markings can be linked in this way, but those that can yield dates of between 1,600 BC to 900 BC. Those carved into natural rock seem to be earlier, while those etched onto megaliths are newer.

The more exposed sections of the boulder at Roughting Linn have weathered badly over the past few thousand years but the cup and ring markings are still clear.

The markings themselves take three forms: cup, ring and channel. Cups are the circular depressions carved into the rock, while rings are the circular markings that are sometimes carved around a cup or sometimes stand alone. There may be as many as 12 rings carved one inside the other. Channels are the grooves that snake off over the surface of the rock in various sinuous curves.

The designs range in complexity, from an isolated cup right up to a vast mass of carvings with dozens of cups and rings linked by extensive channels. On at least one rock the channels were quite clearly carved so as to carry rainwater from one cup to another, on a route that involved more than nine cups. Most markings, however, are not so obviously linked to rainwater movements and some are quite impossible for rainwater to flow along.

A few of the more complex patterns are highly sophisticated and display an advanced knowledge of geometry. The relationships between the depth of cups and their circumference, between the diameters of adjacent rings and the sweep of nearby channels, demonstrate an ability by whoever carved them to measure angles and tangents or to draw ellipses, ovals and circles with great accuracy. Whether this mathematical knowledge was ever used for any practical purpose we do not know. It may have been of use in producing wooden tools, but these have long since rotted away and we are left only with the cup and ring stones. Perhaps the ability to manipulate mathematics in this way was prized only for its usefulness in producing carvings on rock.

The markings are almost always made on the sandstone that underlies much of the county. The reason for this seems to be the way in which they were made. The markings were carved out long before metal chisels were invented, so the only way that they could have been produced was by pounding the boulder with a piece of harder rock. In the case of Northumberland the harder 'hammer rocks' would seem to have been made out of granite or porphyrite from the Cheviots. The vast majority of cup and ring markings seen today have smooth surfaces, but that is due to erosion by water and wind over the past 3,000 years. The few markings that have been protected by soil show the rough surface left by the bashing of the sandstone with granite hammers.

The sites of the markings are nearly always on slopes or hilltops that command sweeping views across the surrounding land. For decades all the ideas about the purpose and function of the cup and ring markings were based on the fact that they were in high places from which anybody standing beside them could see for miles. More recently it has been realised that the rocks on which the markings were carved could be seen from miles around and some new ideas about their purpose have been developed.

The earlier theories tended to emphasise a religious origin for the markings. It was felt that anything that could not be readily explained in practical terms – such as spears or

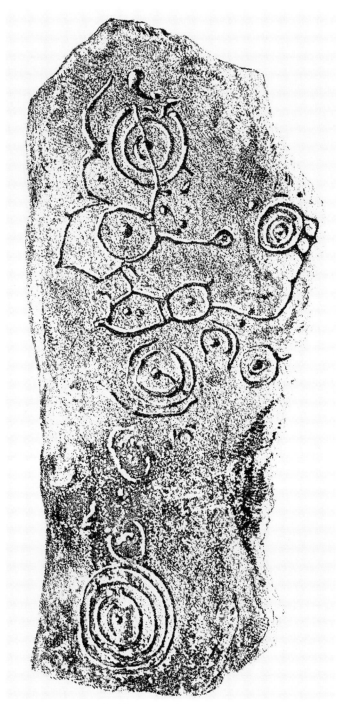

A Victorian engraving of the elaborate cup and ring markings to be found on a standing stone on Broom Ridge.

needles — probably had a ceremonial purpose. These ideas tended to have been first conceived in Victorian times, when religion was rather more important in daily life than it is today, so the ideas may tell us more about the people who developed them than about the cup and ring markings.

There were generally two strands of thought among those who believed that the markings were religious. The first noted the location of the carvings on exposed boulders on hilltops and exposed slopes. It was felt that such locations were ideal for the worship of a deity related to the sky. Priests may have gathered at the stones to make sacrifices to a sun god or a moon goddess. Perhaps the markings might have had some role in channelling blood from a sacrificed sheep, chicken or human.

Other researchers have concentrated on the shapes of the carvings themselves. A temple in Malta, known to have been dedicated to a fertility goddess, was decorated at about this time with circles and spirals. It has been suggested that the cup and ring markings are symbolic of motherhood and fertility. The fact that the carvings were produced by the first farmers in the region might indicate that they were related to the fertility of crops and livestock.

The larger stone slab at Old Bewick, as depicted in a Victorian engraving. The marks have been interpreted in various ways but nobody is really certain what they mean.

More recently, archaeologists have accepted that not all ritual or ceremonial activity is necessarily related to religion. All sorts of activities have rituals associated with them, from the opening of a local village fete to the coronation of a monarch. The fact that the carved stones could be seen from across a wide area might indicate that they had a role in trade, power politics or some other social function. A popular theory is that they marked the presence or territory of a particular tribe or family – that they were, in effect, property markers.

The simple fact remains, however, that for all the years of study that have been devoted to the cup and ring markings we are little further forward in understanding them; they remain an enigmatic mystery.

Given that the cup and ring markings were carved out of the living rock on hilltops, they are not always the most straightforward of features for the visitor to try to find. Probably the most easily accessible is the huge exposed boulder at Roughting Linn, which lies adjacent to the lane that runs to Roughtinglinn farm from Fentonhill, west of Belford. Hare Crag is also fairly easy to reach, lying off the A6111 Wooler to Berwick road, just north of the Wrangham farm. Getting there involves a walk of about 300 yards over rough grazing land. The carved rocks on Bewick Moor above Old Bewick are less easy to find, but are significant as they are linked to burial barrows that help to date them. The rocks lie to the east of a wood on Bewick Hill, some distance from the nearest path and more than a mile from the nearest road.

The cup and ring markings seem to have stopped being made around 1100 BC and by 900 BC no new ones were being produced, nor were established ones any longer being restored or cared for. Instead, they were left to erode away. This change in behaviour occurred about the time that bronze first began to be used. The Bronze Age is something of a misnomer for only the very richest people could afford bronze, most people carried on using stone tools.

As well as abandoning cup and ring markings, the new culture saw people living in a distinct type of dwelling which archaeologists call 'palisaded homes'. These take the form of a round or oval enclosure that covered about an acre, though they varied widely in size and shape. The wall was made of timbers set upright in the ground, forming a stout wooden fence that could easily have withstood any efforts by man or beast to knock it down. Sometimes there was a second palisade outside the first. Within the palisade stood one or more wooden houses, together with other structures that appear to have been granaries, animal barns and agricultural buildings. Some palisaded enclosures lie so close together that the inhabitants could talk to each other easily, while others lie miles from the nearest. Inevitably, the sites of the vast majority of these have been lost over time to erosion, ploughing and other causes.

Then, in around 600 BC, a massive and largely unexplained change came over society in Northumberland. The old palisaded enclosures were abandoned and instead people

The great hill of Yeavering Bell is topped by the largest and most elaborate hill fort in Northumberland. It was almost certainly one of the tribal headquarters of the Votadini Celtic tribe, who lived here in pre-Roman times.

began to live in hill forts. Despite their name, these structures were more like fortified towns, with populations that were often in the hundreds and sometimes numbered in the thousands. They were heavily fortified with deep ditches, high banks and sophisticated wooden or stone walls. Northumberland, it would seem, was becoming a much more dangerous place to live. But why?

One reason may have been an increasing population, which could have made good land scarce and so led to squabbles and fights. However, the new hill forts were generally on a much larger scale than the older palisaded enclosures, meaning that many more people were living together in the same place. This argues for a more sophisticated form of political arrangement than the family or clan-based structure of the Neolithic and Bronze Age. This is not the only sign that things were changing: iron weapons were now in use.

It seems that a new wave of migrants, or at least a new culture, had swept over Northumberland. This time it was the Celtic culture that took over. This culture, and perhaps the people who went with it, had originated in the upper Danube several centuries earlier, but by 600 BC had expanded across most of western Europe, as well as down the Danube and over the Black Sea into what is now Turkey. The Romans knew these people as 'Gauls', the name 'Celt' being that given to them by the Greeks.

In Northumbria the coming of the Celtic culture saw the construction of several dozen small hill forts, around four or six acres in size, and also the building of some massive fortified enclosures. So strong were the defensive positions chosen, that several of them have been reused so often that the original hill fort has been all but obliterated. The fortified sites at Bamburgh, Dunstanburgh and Tynemouth have all been built over by mediaeval castles. Fortunately, the greatest of them all remains untouched: Yeavering Bell.

This huge hill fort was spread over 12 acres of ground and contained around 150 houses, plus associated barns, granaries and the like. The defences consisted of a massive stone and earth rampart some 14 feet thick, which may have stood as high as 30 feet tall when first built. The eastern end contained a smaller area that was separated from the rest of the site by another wall. Perhaps this marked the site of the palace of the ruler of Yeavering Bell. There were two gates through the defences, on the north and south walls, which led into a slight hollow at the centre of the site.

There can be no doubt that hill forts such as Yeavering Bell were easy to defend and provided a secure refuge for its people in times of danger. They were also clearly visible from across a wide area and would have served as very visible marks of the power, might and prestige of the people who lived there.

Not all hill forts were on this scale. The fortification at Brinkburn consisted of an earthen bank and ditch that ran across the promontory of land looped by the River Coquet. There was only one way into the village behind the fortifications and that was through the gateway left in the wooden walls that originally topped the bank. Impressive as these defences were, there do not seem to have been any walls lining the river bank behind them. If the village was subjected to serious attack, an enemy force could quite easily have swum across and outflanked the defences. Perhaps the earthworks and wooden walls were intended more to impress a visitor than to drive off an attacker.

Nor is it very clear whether each hill fort represents the centre for a tribe, or whether only the largest were tribal capitals and the smaller ones outposts or clan residences. What we do know is that by the time the Romans arrived on the scene in AD 80, what is now Northumberland was in the hands of the Votadini, a tribe that ruled the lands from the Tyne to the Forth and from the sea to the Cheviots. The tribe does not seem to have been a centralised kingdom, such as the Iceni and Cantiaci were in the south of Britain, but more in the way of a confederacy of related minor tribal units.

One of the abiding mysteries of the Roman conquest of Britain is what attitude the Votadini held to the Roman invasion. The Romans had landed in Britain more than 30 years earlier and had been gradually extending and consolidating their power ever since. By the time the governor, Julius Agricola, began his push north from York to conquer all of northern Britain, the Votadini would have had several decades to ponder how they would react when the legions came their way.

It is unfortunate, therefore, that the written Roman sources make no mention at all of the Votadini during this campaign. We know that the IX Legion built a fortress at Corbridge on the Tyne to act as a base for operations in the summer of AD 80. One historian states that the fortress was so well built, provisioned and garrisoned that it was never lost through attack or lack of supplies. Whether this means that it was actually attacked or not is not clear. Certainly, none of the hill forts show any sign of having been attacked, burned or looted.

It is possible that the Votadini chose to make peace with the Romans. Agricola, if he followed Roman practice elsewhere, would have given the Votadini generous terms. The nobles would have retained their lands and the right to administer justice and collect taxes as they always had done. Taxes would, of course, have to be paid to Rome and the armed forces disbanded, but otherwise the Votadini would have continued to live as they had done before the Roman advance. It was probably at this time that most of the hill forts were abandoned. In other areas the Romans forced the locals to abandon fortified towns and instead settle in open country, where they could more easily be watched by the Roman patrols. Most locals took to living in stone-walled farmsteads large enough for a single extended family of some 20 or so individuals.

The earthwork that cuts off the ridge of high ground at Brinkburn has survived more or less intact. In Celtic times the bank would have been both taller and steeper, as well as being topped by an impressive wooden defensive wall.

In AD 83 Agricola fought a battle against an alliance of northern tribes at a place he called Mons Graupius (probably Bennachie mountain near Inverurie). He inflicted a defeat on the natives, but most of the Britons escaped and their leaders refused to surrender. There then followed a protracted guerrilla war, which was ended in AD 88 when the XX Legion was withdrawn from Britain to fight a war in Dacia in the East. Short on men, Agricola pulled back to build a frontier on the narrow neck of land between the Forth and the Clyde. This was intended to be a permanent frontier, which left the Votadini clearly within the Roman Empire.

It was not to last and in its collapse lie the origins of the most enigmatic and insoluble mysteries of Roman Britain.

In AD 120 the northern tribes, possibly aided by warriors brought over from Ireland, stormed south. The defences on the Forth-Clyde isthmus collapsed. The then governor of Britain, Quintus Pompeius Falco, ordered the IX Legion to march north to defeat the invasion with the II Legion in support.

What happened next is entirely obscure, and the greatest mystery of all concerns the fate of the IX Legion, one of the premier fighting units of the Roman Empire. The legion vanishes from the written records of the Roman Empire and is never mentioned again.

The usual Roman practice by this date was to keep a legion on a permanent basis, with some of them existing for more than 300 years. The legion might be divided up into smaller units to be stationed at different places if military necessity demanded it, but the legion itself remained in being as a unit, through which wages were paid, rations distributed and promotions made. Even if a legion suffered catastrophic losses in a battle, it would be brought back up to strength as quickly as possible. The disappearance of the IX Legion is unique and is made all the more mysterious by the lack of any reference to its fate in histories or documents. It is as if it simply vanished into thin air.

The IX Legion had never been a particularly lucky unit and in its history there may be clues as to its fate. The IX were raised in 65 BC and sent to campaign in Spain – which probably explains their title of Hispana and their symbol of a bull. Only citizens of Rome were entitled to serve in a legion. Other inhabitants of the Roman Empire could join the auxiliary forces, which very often had specialist roles such as light cavalry, riverboat forces or engineers.

In 61 BC the IX formed part of the army used by Julius Caesar when he was governor of Further Spain. He then moved the IX to Gaul when he became governor there in 58 BC and the legion fought throughout the whole of the subsequent Gallic Wars. The IX remained loyal to Caesar throughout the Roman civil wars and suffered heavy losses. When Caesar was appointed dictator for life, peace appeared to have arrived, so Caesar disbanded the legion and gave its surviving veterans land to farm in Italy.

When Caesar was murdered in 44 BC, his nephew Octavian called upon his uncle's supporters to avenge the killing in a renewed round of civil wars. Nearly all the veterans of the IX volunteered, so Octavian reformed the legion and led it to war. The IX served with distinction and were present at the climactic Battle of Actium in 31 BC. That victory made Octavian ruler of the Roman Empire and he was given the title by which he is better known: Augustus.

The IX Legion were then sent back to Spain to complete the conquest of the peninsula. In 13 BC it moved to the Rhine frontier and was probably involved in campaigns against the various German tribes. In AD 9 it escaped the massacre of three legions at the Battle of the Teutoburg Forest by being in reserve at the time.

In AD 43 the IX joined the Roman invasion of Britain led by Emperor Claudius. Thereafter, they stayed in Britain. At first they were based at Lincoln, then in York and finally at Corbridge. In AD 61 the IX suffered catastrophic losses in the revolt of Queen Boadicea of the Iceni. When the news of the uprising in what is now East Anglia first reached the Romans, the IX at their base in Lincoln were the only unit in a position to intervene, as the other Roman forces were campaigning in North Wales. The commander of the IX, Quintus Petillius Cerialis, had most of his legion with him – some of it was out patrolling the lands to the north – as well as his auxiliary cavalry. He set off to march south to save London. The IX got about as far as Peterborough when they were struck by the full force of the army led by Boadicea. The Iceni had been joined by the Trinovantes and warriors from other tribes. The IX were not only heavily outnumbered, but were caught strung out on the march and so were unable to adopt a proper defensive formation. The legionaries were wiped out in the slaughter that followed and Cerialis escaped with a handful of cavalry.

Despite the annihilation of most of the IX, the legion were reformed after the defeat of Boadicea by drafting in a few veterans from other legions and a mass of raw recruits from the continent. By AD 71, the unit was back to fighting trim and was sent to establish the fortress at Eboracum (York) and to take part in the campaign to subdue the powerful Brigantes tribe, which dominated the Pennines and adjacent areas. The success of that campaign brought the Roman Empire, and the IX Legion, to the southern borders of the Votadini.

During Agricola's northern campaign, the IX suffered another disaster. On the march north that ended at the Battle of Mons Graupius, Agricola detached the IX Legion from the main army to go to deal with a group of Celts reported to be gathering some distance from the main enemy force. It was a ruse to get Agricola to divide his force. The British commander, Calgacus, hurriedly concentrated his main army and attacked the IX at midnight.

The site of this night attack was probably either Pinnata Castra or Lochore, in what is now Fife. The sentries were overrun with ease and the Britons were inside the camp before the alarm was sounded. After some bitter fighting, the Celts forced open the gates, allowing their main force to surge in. Some legionaries tried to flee, but were cut down by units of the enemy posted along the most obvious escape routes. A core of the IX managed to form a defensive perimeter among the tents and settled down to try to hold out against the vastly superior numbers of the enemy.

Meanwhile, a scout, who had been away from the camp when the attack began, had ridden hard to reach Agricola. The Roman commander got his cavalry units on the road and reached the camp of the IX about dawn. There was a desperate fight as the cavalry charged the enemy, but seeing that his hopes of annihilating the IX at little cost were gone, Calgacus called off the battle and slipped away.

The losses to the IX in this action were very heavy, but we have no precise figures. Certainly, the legion played no major part in the rest of the campaign. It seems to have been withdrawn from the fighting altogether and sent south to be reformed once again. They were then moved to York, no doubt with advanced units at Corbridge.

When the barbarian assault of AD 120 began, the northern frontier on the Clyde-Forth line was held by auxiliary units. These occupied a string of forts, which sent out patrols to keep an eye on the tribes to the north and kept in constant touch with the legions to the south. If any trouble threatened, the legions marched north to quell it. The attack of AD 120 was so carefully planned that the unfortunate auxiliaries had no warning that it was coming and so were unable to summon the legions in time to help them. It was only after the barbarians were over the border that word reached York and the IX set off north over the Tyne.

The barbarian attack was not simply an invasion, it was part of a coordinated plan of resistance. It is not entirely clear if the Votadini joined the uprising, though some of them almost certainly did, but the fate of the IX would have been sealed if the Votadini did rise.

Assuming that the uprising of the Votadini did take place and had been prepared as carefully and secretly as the invasion from the north, the IX would have had no warning of the rebellion. They would have marched north along Dere Street from Corbridge to cross the mountains and so reached the auxiliary fortress at what is now Inveresk, east of Edinburgh. They would have been strung out on the march, just as their forebears had been when ambushed by Boadicea 60 years earlier. The result might have been the same: annihilation. This time the IX was not reformed, perhaps the losses this time had been so catastrophic that there were simply not enough men left to form the core of a new legion. Or perhaps the sacred eagle standard of the legion had been captured and was never recovered.

A modern reconstruction of a Celtic farmstead, built at Rochester in the mid-1990s.

However, the fate of the IX Legion is not quite as straightforward as this scenario suggests. Some tiles stamped with the name of the IX Legion have been found at Nijmegan in the Netherlands. The dating of these tiles is not entirely precise, but they do seem to have been made in around AD 121. Also there is the tomb of an officer in the IX Legion, which seems to have been carved in around AD 140. Several historians have used these facts to suggest that the IX was not massacred in Northumbria, but instead survived to be transferred to Nijmegan and continued in existence to at least AD 140. It is suggested that if this were so then it was most likely lost in the disastrous campaign against the Parthians in AD 161. Certainly, the legion had ceased to exist by AD 170, as it does not feature on the army lists for that year, which have survived intact.

However, neither the Nijmegan tiles nor the tomb prove that the legion was in existence then. The makers of the tiles may have been a small detachment from the main force, while the tomb may have belonged to a veteran or to some lucky soul who was detached from the legion when it marched north to its fate.

The most likely solution to the mystery of the disappearance of the elite IX Legion remains that it was wiped out during the northern war of AD 120. Probably somewhere near the fort of Bremenium, now High Rochester.

Whatever the fate of the IX Hispana, the results of the war in AD 120 were clear. Emperor Hadrian arrived in Britain in AD 122 to find the northern frontier in turmoil, the Votadini subdued but truculent and the Clyde-Forth line the scene of fighting. He ordered that the northern lands should be abandoned and a new frontier established on the line of the Tyne-Solway. Along this line Hadrian ordered to be built the wall and chain of fortresses that bears his name down to the present day. The Votadini and most of what is now Northumberland were set free of direct Roman rule, though patrols would continue to move across their lands to keep an eye open for any gathering trouble.

Later tradition would confuse the purpose and origins of the wall. It came to be called the Picts Wall, as it had been built to keep the northern barbarian Picts out of Roman Britain. This was later misunderstood to mean that it had been built by the Picts. A whole host of legendary and mythical tales were developed around this spurious theme.

Once Hadrian's Wall was established it remained a secure frontier for almost all of the four centuries that the Roman Empire ruled Britain. Only after AD 350 was there any real trouble and most of that involved raiders in ships sailing down the coast to bypass the wall, rather than invasions over it. However, in AD 410 the Roman Empire was crumbling, the legions were withdrawn and the Emperor Honorius sent back a message. He told the assorted civitates of Britain that they had to look after their own defence. These civitates were part of the local government that lay under the governor appointed by the emperor. Clearly, the governor had gone with the legions. The Romano-Britons were on their own, and the way was made clear for two of the most shadowy and mysterious figures of the period known as the Dark Ages.

The first of these to emerge is today known largely from his role in a nursery rhyme: Old King Cole.

Roman stonework at High Rochester. This was a small fort built as an advance line of defence from Hadrian's Wall. The IX Legion may have been marching north along the old Roman road to the Forth that passes this point when it was ambushed by a force of Votadini tribesmen and cut to pieces, but the unit's ultimate fate remains a mystery.

A stretch of Hadrian's Wall near Corbridge. Later generations would forget that the wall had been built by the Romans to keep out the Picts and would instead ascribe its construction to Picts, giants and fairies. Many aspects of the wall's construction and use remain mysteries to this day.

The rhyme was first recorded in 1708 and then ran:

'Old King Cole was a merry old soul

And a merry old soul was he;

He called for his pipe, and he called for his bowl

And he called for his fiddlers three.

Every fiddler he had a fiddle,

And a very fine fiddle had he;

Oh there's none so rare, as can compare

With King Cole and his fiddlers three.'

The rhyme refers back to a king of legendary fighting abilities, who is recorded in many histories from the Middle Ages as having lived several generations earlier and who was the founder of several royal dynasties among the British kingdoms that sprang up as Roman Britain collapsed in chaos. He is variously called Coel Hen (Coel the Old) or Coel Godhebog (Coel the Defender). Counting back through the generations, from known dates in the lists of ancestors, gives a date for the reign of Cole of about 420 or 440. The name of Coel is almost certainly derived from the Roman name Coelius. Most of the documents agree that Coel married a woman named Stradwawl and had three children, two sons named Garmonion and Cunedda II and a daughter named Wawl.

The main mystery surrounding King Coel is whether or not he actually existed, and if he did then who was he.

The oldest sources that refer to Coel were written about 500 years after he was supposed to have lived, though they do claim to be copies of documents about 200 years older than that. This still means that the oldest sources relating to Coel were written some 300 years after he lived. Casting further doubt on his reality is that the name of his wife translates from an old version of Welsh to be 'Road on the Wall', while the name of his daughter means simply 'Wall'. Clearly both refer to the Hadrian's Wall that dominated the landscape of the north and are almost certainly legendary. It is, therefore, tempting to believe that Coel did not really exist.

However, there are factors in Coel's favour. The various ancestor lists all put his lifespan in a fairly consistent time frame, which would not be expected of a mythical ancestor figure. Moreover, the fact that several different royal dynasties claimed descent from him would indicate that he had been a figure of real importance, who bestowed legitimacy and prestige on his descendants. In addition, all the royal houses who claimed Coel as an ancestor were grouped between the Forth and the Humber.

If Coel had been a real person he must have ruled the lands from the Forth to the Humber around the year 420. Had there been such a man?

The ruins of a milecastle on Hadrian's Wall near to Corbridge. The nursery rhyme favourite Old King Cole may have been the last of the Roman commanders to have control of the wall. Later tradition said that his daughter was named 'Wall'.

Surprising as it may sound, there had. In the defence of Roman Britain in the fourth century, the lands from the Forth to Hadrian's Wall were commanded by a military officer who held the rank of Dux Britanniarum, 'Duke of the Britains'. In this context, the title of Dux was a Roman rank roughly equivalent to that of a modern military general. The Dux Britanniarum had command of not only regular Roman troops but also auxiliaries, local militia and barbarian mercenaries hired from outside the Empire.

When Honorius pulled out, temporarily as everyone at the time thought, the regular soldiers were withdrawn to defend Rome. That left the Dux Britanniarum with his local militia, hired mercenaries and, perhaps, the auxiliaries. His task remained the same: defend the prosperous southern civitates against raids launched by the northern barbarians.

We know that the civitates at first banded together and pooled their resources both for defence and to continue the imperial administration of Britain. Everybody believed that the crisis facing Rome was merely temporary. The British wanted to be ready for the return of imperial rule when it came. It was not until many years later, exactly how many is open to dispute, that people began to realise that the Roman Empire was finished and that a new future beckoned.

The Dux Britanniarum was made answerable to a new 'High Ruler', elected by a council made up of the leaders of the various civitates. There can be no doubt that the Dux Britanniarum and his men were paid out of taxes raised in the civitates. Archaeological evidence shows that the wall and its fortresses were manned, albeit by reduced numbers of troops, for some decades after 410.

This might explain why the 'Road along the Wall' and the 'Wall' were made by later chroniclers to be the wife and daughter of Coel. In a later age, Emperor Napoleon of France called his mobile artillery 'my beautiful daughters' and similar nicknames are not uncommon. Perhaps Coel really did call the wall his 'daughter'.

The man who held the position of Dux Britanniarum after 410 will undoubtedly have come from the ruling Romano-British elite and almost certainly had served in the Roman army. He would probably have had a Roman name, even if he was British by birth. Coelius would be a very believable name for this man, though in truth we do not know his name from any contemporary source.

When the post-Roman system broke down, Coelius or his successor would have been left as ruler of the lands previously administered by the Dux Britanniarum. In the face of barbarian pressure, it would have made sense for this military state to continue in existence for so long as the incoming Scots, Picts and Angles could be held off. The state may have been divided up between Coel's sons and grandsons, as the ancestor lists claim. If this were the case, the new dynasties would have based their right to rule on descent from the last man to have been officially appointed by legitimate Roman authority: Old King Cole himself.

By the year 500 or thereabouts the lands of the Dux Britanniarum had been divided into Rheged to the west of the Pennines, York and Kynelyn, which was located north of the Tyne. These three kingdoms would survive until the coming of the English, which in itself was something of a mystery.

Whatever the truth about Coel, the mystery surrounding him pales into insignificance beside the controversies that have swirled around the other mysterious figure of the Dark Ages: King Arthur.

Unlike Coel, the name Arthur is probably a Celtic one: Artoros. If he existed at all, and some historians state quite clearly that he did not, he lived about the year 490. By this date the disintegration of post-Roman Britain had moved on from Coel's day. By 490, several groups of Germanic mercenaries had successfully rebelled and established fledgling kingdoms of their own that were independent of the authority of the Romano-Britons. These were the kingdoms of Kent, Sussex and East Anglia, with perhaps Deira in southern Yorkshire as well. Increasing numbers of Saxons and Angles were pouring over the North Sea in search of land and wealth.

Meanwhile, the economy of Roman Britain had collapsed. The silver mines, lead mines and the farms that had employed tens of thousands of men had gone. They had relied on exporting their products to the rest of the Empire and that had now collapsed. Instead, post-Roman Britain was reduced to an economy based on subsistence agriculture with limited amounts of small-scale industrial output in the shape of tin mining in Cornwall, pottery workshops and the like.

However, although their economy and wealth had vanished, the Britons clung to their Christian religion and their Roman heritage. Many people continued to live in ageing and increasingly patched up Roman houses, complete with mosaics, heating systems and brick walls. Towns may have declined in population, but they still existed, and the civitates system of government was still going. A 'High Ruler' was still being elected to fulfil the functions of the long-vanished emperor, the most important of which was to lead the combined armed forces of the Britons.

In the year 495 (or 516 depending on how you read the chronologies) the Germanic incomers made a major effort to smash the fragile unity of the civitates system. It seems that all the English kingdoms mustered their men and marched to war, launching a strike deep into the wealthiest parts of post-Roman Britain in the southern civitates around the Thames Valley. We know that this major campaign ended at the Battle of Badon Hill in a crushing defeat over the invaders. Thereafter, there followed many years of peace in

Britain. There could be no return to Roman prosperity and British weakness continued, despite the great victory at Badon.

We also know that about 25 years after Badon, the civitates and high ruler system of government had collapsed and Christianity was on the decline. Power in most civitates was grabbed by military hard men, but they were unable to resist a resurgent English power. By 600 most of what is now England was in the hands of the English.

Histories and chronicles written 300 years later credit the victory at Badon to 'Arthur', a leader said to have fought a series of 12 battles against the English. He was also said to have been killed along with 'Medraut' in the Battle of Camlann, apparently a struggle between rival Romano-British forces.

As with Coel, the problem is first to decide whether or not Arthur existed and then, if he did, to try to fit him alongside the known events of the time. Unlike Coel, Arthur is not claimed as an ancestor to any dynasty of rulers. This might, at first glance, seem to reduce the chances of his having been a real person. However, the list of battles he is said to have fought in puts at least four of the 12 in what is now Lincolnshire. This area was a stronghold of the Britons and held out against the English long after the rest of eastern Britain succumbed. However, when it did fall the records of its ruling dynasty and history were lost. All that was preserved was a list of the kings who ruled there from about 570 to 730 when the kingdom fell. These kings were: Cretta, Cuelgils, Caedbaed, Bubba, Beda, Biscop, Eanfer and Eatta. If Arthur had been from Lincoln, as the list of battles suggests, his links to the dynasty of that area would have been lost in the English conquest.

Another weakness for Arthur is that he is not mentioned by name in any documents that have any claim to be contemporary with his supposed lifetime in around the year 500. However, these documents mention very few names at all, instead preferring to talk about events. The sole contemporary reference to the Battle of Mount Badon, for instance, does not say who commanded the Romano-Britons. Clearly, somebody commanded them and later histories stated it was Arthur.

There seems little genuine reason to doubt that Arthur existed or that he led the Britons to their great victory at Badon. However, if his great victory was fought in the south, probably near Bath, and he himself came from Lincolnshire, what has he to do with Northumberland?

In fact, there are many ties between the mysterious figure of Arthur and Northumbria. The list of Arthur's battles places one of them in the forests north of Hadrian's Wall, while a second was put at 'the city of the legions', which might have been Chester, Carlisle or York. Clearly, Arthur was campaigning as far north as Northumberland.

A more direct link comes in the form of an old story from Sewingshields, on the banks of the Derwent. The tale tells of a shepherd who tended his sheep over these hills three or more centuries ago. While his sheep grazed peacefully, he spent his time knitting himself some winter stockings. When he accidentally dropped the ball of wool, it bounced off down the hillside at quite a pace. Putting down his knitting, the man set off to retrieve it.

Following the thread, the shepherd found that the ball had run down into a particularly dense patch of brambles and long grass. Squirming carefully into the thicket, the man found himself confronted by a doorway set into the side of the hill. The dense foliage cast an eerie green light over the scene, but, not daunted, the shepherd decided to explore; his wool forgotten.

Giving the door a gentle push, the shepherd felt it move so he pushed harder and the ancient door opened on rusty hinges to reveal a passage cut into the stone of the hill. A rush of bats made the shepherd start back, but once they were gone he pushed on. The floor of the passage was alive with toads, but still he crept on into the darkness. Feeling his ways warily with his hands and feet, the shepherd progressed slowly. Then he saw ahead of him a faint light that grew brighter as he moved closer.

Turning a corner, the shepherd emerged into a great cavern that was lit by a magical fire of pure white flames leaping up from a crack in the floor. Beside the fire was a great table on which rested a sword in its scabbard, a garter and a hunting horn. Behind the table sat a king bedecked in a richly furred robe encrusted with jewels and with a crown on his head. The king was asleep, breathing deeply and evenly. On a second chair sat a beautiful woman, whom the shepherd took to be the queen. Around the chamber were ranged other chairs and couches on which slumbered dozens of men and women.

The shepherd had heard tales about King Arthur and in particular the story that said that King Arthur was not dead but merely sleeping a magical sleep. When conditions were right, the legend said, Arthur would return to rule Britain and the kingdom would know happiness and prosperity once again. The shepherd believed that the sleeping king he saw was Arthur and the other sleepers were Queen Guinevere together with the Knights of the Round Table and their ladies.

The shepherd was scared, but as the sleepers slumbered on peacefully he gradually lost his fear and gingerly stepped forward to investigate. His eyes were caught by the sword on the table, which must surely have been Excalibur. The hilt was richly encrusted with jewels and glimmered as if it were pure gold. Thinking that the sword must be worth a great deal of money, more if it were Excalibur, the shepherd decided to take it.

He reached forward and grabbed the sword hilt, pulling it from its scabbard. As he did so the king suddenly sat upright on his chair and opened his eyes. The startled shepherd promptly dropped the sword in fright. As the blade fell it cut the garter, whereupon all the knights and ladies began to stretch and yawn as they awoke. Hurriedly grabbing the sword again, the shepherd slammed it back into its scabbard, causing the king and knights to fall back asleep.

Taking to his heels, the shepherd ran out of the chamber and back along the corridor. As he fled, the shepherd heard a mighty voice booming out behind him shouting:

'Oh, woe betide the evil day

On which this witless wight was born,

Who drew the sword, the garter cut,

But never blew the bugle horn.'

Soon the shepherd was out the door and alone on the hillside. He grabbed his discarded ball of wool and hurriedly drove the flock of sheep to fresh pastures. Later that night, the shepherd began to regret what he had done. He recalled that the tales had said that Arthur would return to make Britain a happy and prosperous kingdom once again. The shepherd decided to go back the next day so that he could blow the horn as well as draw the sword and cut the garter. However, no matter how hard he searched he was never able to find the ancient door behind the thicket. And so, it is said, King Arthur slumbers yet beneath the hills of Sewingshields.

What to make of the mix of legend and history is a conundrun indeed. Some historians believe that Arthur was merely a mythical figure with no basis in reality, while others credit him with having been a real person, but claim there is not enough evidence to fix him securely in place or time. This does not mean, however, that the mystery cannot be solved.

It is not beyond the bounds of reason that Arthur did lead the Romano-British forces to victory at Badon as later chronicles state. If so, he was in a position to bring together the military forces of the assorted civitates of the period. Only one person had the power to do this: the high ruler elected by the council. Unfortunately, the records for the men who held this position are incomplete.

The first high ruler was a man named Gwrtheyn, son of Vitalis of Glevum, who took up his office in around 415 or so. Gwrtheyn is a British name, but Vitalis is Roman and Glevum is the Roman name for Gloucester. This Gwrtheyn is better known by his title of Vortigern, the British words for high ruler. It was he who lost Kent and East Anglia to the Germanic mercenaries when they rose in rebellion about the year 449. Gwrtheyn then lost power to a man with the solidly Roman name of Ambrosius Aurelianus. This ruler is said to have fought the English, not terribly successfully. He also reorganised the civitates system by appointing the leader of each civitates to be a consul. If the name retained its Roman meaning at this time, the move may have been an attempt to replace the civilian council with a more military hierarchy.

The records then become confused. Ambrosius died, or resigned his position, around 476 but it is not clear what happened next. He may have been succeeded by his brother, who had the equally Roman name of Victorus, rendered into British as Uthor; or his death may have marked the end of the position of high ruler; or perhaps he may have been replaced

The mighty fortress rock of Bamburgh is recorded as the base for the enigmatic Anglian warlord named Ida in the year 547. Although he is recorded as the founder of English power in the north, almost nothing about Ida is known for certain.

by Arthur. If Arthur did follow Ambrosius or Uthor, then his position as high ruler would have given him the power to muster the armies of the Romano-Britons for war.

If the later histories are correct in stating that Arthur was killed at Camlann in a civil war some 30 years after Badon it might explain a lot. The British state almost immediately collapsed into petty, feuding cities, ruled by upstart generals and dictators. Within two generations, these were swept away by the invading English and the British were reduced to a condition of slavery in England. Any people faced by such a disaster will naturally look back to the good old days when things were viewed as much better. The last time that the Britons had things their own way had been under the last of the high rulers: Arthur. This was why later legends and tales clustered around Arthur and why he was remembered long after Ambrosius and Gwrtheyn were forgotten. He may not have been the best or the greatest, but he was the last.

After the collapse of the post-Roman state, Northumberland became part of the kingdom of Kynelyn. Then, in 547, disaster struck. The mighty Roman fortress of Bamburgh fell into the hands of an Anglian warlord named Ida. This Ida is a mystery. An early genealogy composed perhaps 50 years after he died lists his ancestors and makes him the great-great-great-great-grandson of Woden, the leader of the pagan German gods. A divine ancestry is unlikely – though you never know. In any case, no document says where he came from and it seems that within 50 years of his death nobody knew. He may have come from the Anglian homelands in northern Germany, or he may have already been employed as a mercenary somewhere in Britain. We simply do not know.

The battlefield of Heavenfield, where in 635 King Oswald of Northumbria defeated an invasion led by the pagan King Cadwalla of Mercia. The chapel marks the site of the burial pit where the Christian dead were interred.

Nor is it clear what he was doing in Bamburgh. The oldest source states simply that he arrived in Bamburgh in 547, founded the royal dynasty of the Northumbrians and ruled for 12 years. It is not clear if he had founded a kingdom, or was a bandit based in an impregnable stronghold. He may even have been a mercenary hired by the kings of Kynelyn, whose importance was exaggerated by his more powerful descendants.

If Ida of Bamburgh remains a mystery, his son Athelric is even more so. Nothing is known of him except his name and the fact that he too lived at Bamburgh. Things become a little clearer with his alleged grandson, Athelferth. Athelferth is said to have become king in Bamburgh in 593, so perhaps he was Ida's great-grandson given the average lifespan at the time. It was Athelferth who formed an alliance with the English of Deira, what is now southern Yorkshire. Together they conquered York, breaking the power of one of the three British kingdoms in the north. Progress was then rapid and within a generation the English ruled all of Northumberland, as well as most of the territory from the Humber to the Forth. The kingdom of Northumbria had been founded.

In 635 Northumbria faced a threat to its independence when the pagan King Cadwalla of Mercia led an army to invade and conquer. Northumbria was, at the time, in the hands of a young and untried prince named Oswald. Just before the two armies clashed, Oswald erected a wooden cross and ordered his entire army to kneel and pray for victory over the pagan. The battle was won and the site quickly renamed Heavenfield. The cross has since been replaced by a small chapel, which is open to the public most days.

Oswald soon became an ideal Christian ruler. One day he was sitting down to lunch with Bishop Aidan of Lindisfarne when the steward interrupted to say that a crowd of beggars were outside asking for food. He asked permission to send out the unwanted kitchen scraps. Oswald refused and instead ordered the steward to take the royal meal outside for the beggars, adding that the silver platter on which it was being served should be cut up and distributed as well. Aidan, later to be made a saint himself, was astonished at the generosity. He flung himself down on his knees, grabbed Oswald's right hand and declared, 'May this hand never perish.'

Some years later Oswald had to face Cadwalla's son and successor in battle at Oswestry, Shropshire. This time the victory went to the pagans. As he fought, Oswald was surrounded by his enemies. He lifted his arms to pray, but a savage blow from a pagan sword severed Oswald's right arm at the shoulder. Another sliced off his head. When the Northumbrians received their dead king's body for burial they kept the head and arm to serve as religious relics. The head was put into the tomb of the great northern saint, St Cuthbert, while the arm was put in a silver casket and sent to Lindisfarne.

When the Viking wars began, the silver casket was opened and the holy arm of Oswald was found to be as fresh as it had been on the day it was interred. This was widely held to be a miracle and the arm was carried away from Lindisfarne by monks for safe keeping. It ended up at Bamburgh where it became the focus for pilgrimage. When King Henry

A broken fragment of a stone cross; part of the monument put up in around 750 to replace the wooden cross erected by King Oswald to mark the site of his victory at Heavenfield.

The modern stone bridge at Battle Bridge, which is thought to have been the site of a conflict between Halfdan and his Vikings and the forces of the wily King Ricsige of Northumbria in the year 875.

VIII closed down the monasteries during the Protestant Reformation of the 16th century, he also ordered the closure of chapels and reliquaries maintained by monasteries. The small chapel containing Oswald's arm was one of these. However, when Henry's soldiers came to take possession of the silver casket and the arm inside it, they found that both had gone missing, along with the monk who looked after them. The monk had, it was said, taken the relic to a safe hiding place. Where that was nobody ever knew and neither monk nor sacred arm have ever been found. They are thought to remain somewhere near Bamburgh.

The fall of York was to be instrumental in the destruction of the kingdom of Northumberland some three centuries later, but once again the events are clouded in mystery. By 867 Christian Northumbria had already been subjected to 70 years of intermittent attacks by the pagan Vikings. The Northumbrians had, on the whole, fared fairly well. Several coastal monasteries, villages and towns had been plundered, but the Vikings had failed to penetrate far inland.

However, King Osbriht of Northumbria was then ousted by a group of nobles led by a man named Aelle. Both claimants to the throne gathered armies and prepared for civil war. It was at that point that a huge Viking army led by Danes named Ivar the Boneless and Halfdan pounced. The Viking force marched toward York where it was met by the combined forces of Osbriht and Aelle, who had joined forces to meet this new threat. There followed a savage battle in which both Osbriht and Aelle were killed, along with most of their men. The Vikings then stormed into York and pillaged it mercilessly.

What is now Yorkshire fell to the Vikings, who installed a puppet king named Egbert and proceeded to strip the land of its wealth. Northumberland was different, but mystery surrounds exactly what happened. It seems certain that an English ruler named Ricsige took power in the northern part of Northumbria and waged an on-off guerrilla war for several years. The details of this conflict have been lost as the Vikings kept no written records themselves and destroyed any that they did find.

We know that in 875 Halfdan arrived in the Tyne with a sizeable army and set out to crush Ricsige. The English avoided a major battle, instead retreating into the hills with their livestock. One battle is thought to have taken place at Battle Bridge and to have ended in a convincing Viking victory. Otherwise, the campaign seems to have been one of raid and counter-raid.

How long Ricsige and his men managed to hold out is unrecorded. His independent English state in Northumberland seems to have vanished by around 910. Whether the Vikings won a military victory or agreed some sort of alliance is unknown. The importance of Ricsige and his mysterious kingdom is that he kept a sword in the back of the Vikings, which proved to be a constant distraction for them during their campaigns to complete the conquest of southern England. It was Alfred the Great, King of Wessex, who finally stopped the Viking advance and laid the foundations for the later unification of England into one kingdom. It is doubtful if he could have achieved what he did without the mysterious Ricsige and his Northumberland warriors lurking in the mists of the hills, and now all but lost to time.

It may be to this unsettled time that the story of the sleeping hero of Dunstanburgh belongs. The story states that the Lord of Dunstanburgh was a good Christian knight beset by pagan enemies – which would fit the period of the Viking wars. He was put under an evil spell by a pagan magician, who was unable to kill the lord due to his Christian faith. Instead, the magician forced the unfortunate knight down into a cave hidden within the massive rocky headland on which Dunstanburgh stands. There his hands were bound with a magical rope, his sword was trapped in its sheath and his hunting horn blocked. The Lord of Dunstanburgh, it is said, remains trapped in his cavern, waiting for some bold hero to break in and rescue him.

Once the Vikings were defeated, the kingdoms that they had carved out for themselves were subdued by the descendants of Alfred the Great into a united Kingdom of England. For a time there was relative peace in Northumberland, but then the various kingdoms to the north were united into Scotland and Northumberland became the war-savaged borderland between the two kingdoms of Great Britain.

Time after time, the same pattern repeated itself in the relations between the two kingdoms. First the Scots would come raiding over the border; stealing cattle, looting villages, raping women and killing men. At first the raids were small in scale and minor in scope, but then the Scots would get bolder. The king of England would protest to the king of the Scots. Depending upon the mood of the northern monarch, the protests might be ignored or a few possessions returned and some payments made. However, the Scots would grow bolder still, launching longer and more numerous raids. By then the king of England would have lost all patience and would lead an invasion on Scotland. The English king would always have more men and money at his command than the Scottish, so the English would win any major battle with great ease and massive slaughter. Scottish villages and towns would go up in flames as the vengeful English marched across the northern kingdom. However, Scotland was too vast and too poor to be worth the cost of conquering and holding, so the English would march back over the border and for some decades all would be quiet.

Then a new generation of young men would grow up in Scotland, who knew nothing of the vast resources of war that could be summoned by the English king, but who could see the rich pickings to be had over the border. They would launch a small raid with success. They would grow bolder and the whole cycle would begin again. Many of

Somewhere beneath the ruins of Dunstanburgh Castle there is said to be sleeping an heroic English warrior, who was imprisoned here by a pagan magician working for the Vikings.

the mysterious tales relating to the past in Northumberland belong to those savage cycles of raids and warfare.

One such story concerns Brinkburn Priory, which lies secluded in a deep ravine inside a loop of the River Coquet. An army of Scottish raiders were plundering their way down Coquet Dale, setting fire to villages and farms as they went. The monks knew that their holy vocation would not save them from the attentions of the Scots, for gold and silver from crosses and reliquaries were as valuable as that from any other source. Nor had the Scots any fear of divine retribution, nor respect for God's property. The monks hid fearfully in their sheltered valley, hoping that the passing raiders would leave them alone.

The main doorway to Brinkburn Priory, which has a mysterious tale attached to it about Scottish raiders in the Middle Ages.

One by one new columns of smoke rose into the air, marking the villages that the Scots passed through. Then the villages further away began to go up in flames, while the smoke from those closer to hand faded away as the flames died down. The Scots had passed on.

The prior fell to his knees in grateful prayer and ordered his brethren to prepare to celebrate a mass of thanksgiving to God for their escape. As monks filed into the church, one younger brother, who was less worldly than the others, ran to ring the great bell that customarily marked the beginning of a service at Brinkburn. He pulled on the rope and the bell sounded out.

A mile away, a straggling group of Scottish scouts heard the bell tolling. They realised that it could mean that a village or settlement had escaped the attentions of their fellow raiders. Determined not to miss out on this chance, the invaders spurred their horses toward the sound of the bell.

Back at Brinkburn, the prior dragged the monk from the bell rope and silenced the ringing, but it was too late: the Scots were already galloping down the lane that led to the priory. In desperation the monks fled, swimming the waters of the Coquet to escape. Behind them, the Scots plundered the priory, torched the buildings and went on their way with their loot.

What happened to the fateful bell is something of a mystery. Some say that the fire started by the Scots burned through the timbers holding the bell in the tower and sent it crashing to the ground to roll into the Coquet. Another version states that when the monks returned, they themselves threw the bell into the river to punish it for having betrayed them to the enemy. Yet another tale says that the monks put the bell into the river to save it from any future marauders. In all versions the fateful bell ended up in the Coquet and there, it is said, it remains to this day.

A very similar tale is told about Blanchland Abbey, except in this version of the story the Scots became lost in a fog and could not find the abbey. One monk, who was hiding out in the heather, overheard the leader of the raiding party announce that they were giving up the hunt and returning to Scotland. The monks then waited until the next day before holding their service of thanksgiving and ringing their bell. Unfortunately, the Scots had got so lost in the fog that they had ridden around in circles. Instead of being miles away on the way back to Scotland, they were only a couple of hundred yards from the abbey. They heard the bells and fell upon the holy community, killing the abbot and stealing everything of value.

Another raid ended less happily for the Scots. They had come down the coast to find a sizeable force of English knights holed up in Bamburgh Castle. The Scots knew that they could not advance any further and leave this force in their rear to ambush them on the way

Blanchland Abbey was one of the more prosperous Northumberland abbeys during the mediaeval period. The bells that rang out from this tower feature in a mysterious tale from the days of Scottish raids into England.

home or to attack their lines of supply, but neither had they brought with them much in the way of heavy siege equipment. Therefore, they decided to try to bluff the English into surrender.

The Scots mustered their army on a small hill to the south-east of Bamburgh Castle and put on an impressive display of formation marching, communal singing and bloodthirsty chanting, while all the time waving their banners and brandishing their weapons and shields. It was a terrifying sight that had struck fear into many an enemy before. It was then that the heralds went forward to demand the surrender of Bamburgh, promising bloodshed and merciless barbarity on the defenders if they did not open the gates immediately.

However, the English were not to be cowed so easily. They had spotted the lack of siege equipment and so they sent the Scottish heralds back with a message of defiance.

The Scottish army received the message with anger. They glowered over at the castle, and then turned for home without the extensive plunder that they had hoped for. The next day the English came out and gleefully renamed the hill 'Glower Over Them' in celebration of the Scots impotent rage. It is still known as Glororum.

To these days of border warfare belongs the tale of Long Lonkin and Lord Wearie. There are various versions of the tale but one of the more consistent names Nafferton as the home of the skilled stonemason Lonkin, known as Long Lonkin because of his gangling long legs and great height. Long Lonkin fell in love with a farmer's beautiful daughter, but she was well aware of her charms and was determined to make the most of them. She had her sights set higher than a skilled mason. Therefore, she spurned Lonkin's attentions and soon attracted the admiration of Lord Wearie of Welton Hall. The pair were married.

A few years later, Lord Wearie decided that his property was not adequately fortified against raiding Scots, so he hired the best mason in the district – Long Lonkin – to improve the defences. Lonkin went to work with his customary skill and produced a structure that could not be captured except by an army with the very latest siege equipment and plenty of time to employ it. However, Lord Wearie quibbled over the bill and refused to pay what he had promised.

Unknown to his many clients, Lonkin always included in the apparently impregnable structures that he built a secret entrance just wide enough for a single man to gain access. He had intended to fund his old age by selling the secrets of these entrances to whoever would pay the highest price. However, with a double grievance against Lord Wearie – for having stolen his sweetheart and refusing to pay the bill – Lonkin decided to use the hidden entrance to Welton Hall himself.

First, Lonkin set about seducing the nurse who cared for the Wearies' newborn baby son. With the nurse well and truly under his influence, Lonkin made an appointment to visit her secretly one night, entering by way of his secret door. On that fatal night, Lonkin persuaded the nurse to lead him to the bedchamber of Lord and Lady Wearie. Once there, Lonkin drew a long dagger and plunged it into the sleeping form of Lady Wearie, then he turned on the baby in the cradle and killed him as well. Lord Wearie was absent, so Long Lonkin took to his heels and fled.

When Lord Wearie returned home he found the scene of slaughter in the bedroom. Distraught with grief though he was, Wearie gave chase. He and his men caught up with Long Lonkin as the latter was hiding in a tree which overhung a deep pool in the Whittle Burn. One version says that Lonkin threw himself into the pool and drowned, another that he was captured and hanged while the nurse was burned at the stake.

What makes the story rather odd is that Nafferton pele tower fell into ruin about a hundred years before Welton Hall was built, making it impossible for the owners of the two places to have been engaged in a feud. However, Lonkin is not depicted as if he were rich enough to live in a tower, so perhaps that part of the tale is incorrect. Or perhaps he lived there when it was a ruin.

Throughout all these centuries of warfare and raiding, the English side of the border was guarded and protected by a small number of wealthy and warlike families, who used the rents gathered from their lands to pay for arms, armour and men. Patrols were sent into the hills and guards posted in the valleys to keep watch for the Scots. Of the various families, none were so old or so grand as the Percy family of Alnwick. The founder of the family, William de Percy, came over to England with William the Conqueror in 1066 and was given land in Yorkshire and Lincolnshire. His descendants achieved fame and glory through both war and politics, and their descendants still live in Alnwick Castle as the dukes of Northumberland.

At some time in the 14th century, one of the daughters of the then Lord Percy was a famous beauty. She was known as the nut-brown maid due to her lustrous, brown hair that was generally reckoned to be her greatest asset. One day there came to Alnwick a young knight taking part in a joust, and who carried a coat of arms that nobody recognised, not even the herald. His identity was a mystery and he seemed to prefer it that way. Still, the young knight was courteous enough and performed well in the jousting. He was a popular guest and soon caught the eye of the nut-brown maid. Before long the two were deeply in love. Lord Percy noticed the romance and decided to discover the young man's true identity before things went too far. Servants and friends were sent out to search the country for clues.

A few days later, the young knight appeared at dawn outside the chamber of the nut-brown maid. He was clearly upset and just as obviously ready to travel. He told his sweetheart that his identity was about to be revealed and that he must therefore flee, never to return. The girl was understandably upset and asked why he had to leave in such a hurry.

Alnwick Castle is the hereditary home of the ancient Percy family, who feature in so many of the odd and mysterious stories about Northumberland.

'I have committed a crime of great shame,' the young knight told her. 'And my life is forfeit to the law. I must go before your father discovers who I am.'

The nut-brown maid told him that she did not care what he had done and declared that she would flee with him. The knight said that this was impossible as he had to take to the wild forests to live as an outlaw; the girl said she was willing to do so. The knight said that the life would be dangerous; she said she did not care. He said it would be uncomfortable and that she would have to learn how to use a bow and knife to hunt wild animals; she said that she would do her best. She was willing to do anything to be with her love.

At last the girl persuaded the young knight to take her with him. Together they rode off into the mists of dawn and headed south-west towards the wild uplands of the Pennines. When he heard that the pair had gone, Lord Percy was furious. This fury soon turned to puzzlement when a messenger came back later that day to tell him who the young knight actually was. He mustered his bodyguard and set off south-west at a brisk pace. He led them over the Pennines to the stronghold of the Earl of Westmoreland and there found his daughter happily married to the son of the earl.

'Why did you behave as you did?' thundered Percy when he met the young knight.

'I wanted to know that your daughter loved me for myself,' came the reply, 'not for my wealth or my titles or because you approved the match.'

Another story relating to the Percy family can be pinpointed to 25 April 1464. The first round in the Wars of the Roses had ended a few months earlier when Edward, Duke of York, had defeated the forces of the Lancastrians and had himself crowned as King Edward IV. However, the great Northumberland fortresses of Alnwick, Bamburgh, Hexham, Bywell, Dunstanburgh and Langley remained in the hands of the Lancastrians. The attitude of King James III of Scotland would be vital if the castles were to remain supplied, so Edward sent a delegation north to talk to the Scottish king and gain his support.

Edward's ambassadors reached Newcastle with an escort of 80 knights and men-at-arms, plus a few hundred archers led by Lord Montagu, younger brother of the mighty Earl of Warwick. News of the small size of the escort reached Sir Ralph Percy, second son of Henry Percy, Earl of Northumberland. Sir Ralph was young, dashing and hugely popular in the North. Unlike his father and elder brother, he supported the Lancastrian cause. He sent out word that he was mustering an army and some 2,000 men gathered at Wooler. There Percy was joined by Lord Roos and Lord Hungerford, each with a thousand men.

Percy positioned his army astride the road north, now the A697 on Hedgeley Moor, where a boggy stream ran across the road and provided an excellent defensive position. Unknown to him, however, Montagu had massively reinforced his escort and was now heading north with around 5,000 men.

The two armies clashed on 25 April, just before noon. The battle began with a shower of arrows and then Montagu's men-at-arms surged forward to get to grips with the Lancastrians. The fighting was savage and in less than half an hour Lord Hungerford's men had fled. They were shortly followed by those of Lord Roos. They had been expecting to ambush a small force, not fight a pitched battle, so their actions are rather understandable.

The local Northumberland men of Sir Ralph Percy, however, stood firm. It was only as the Yorkists got on to their flank that Percy's men edged back from the stream. Gradually, the Yorkists got the upper hand, pushing Percy and his men back against the slopes of Scotia Hill. It was here that the battle reached its climax.

Percy realised that the battle was lost, but then saw an opportunity to win the victory. Montagu was in the front rank urging his men on, when a push by Percy's men left him momentarily isolated. Percy thought that if he could kill Montagu the Yorkists might lose heart and flee. He clapped his spurs into the flanks of his war horse and pushed forward. In a desperate effort to reach his enemy, Percy made his horse leap forward over the front ranks of his own men. It was a gigantic leap, but the gallant effort failed. Percy was dragged from his horse and pinned to the ground with a bill. Seeing their leader dead, the Lancastrians threw down their arms and surrendered.

Much of the battle is known as fact from contemporary chronicles, but great mystery surrounds the mighty 'Percy's Leap' and quite where it took place. Tradition has it that as soon as the battle was over, Lord Montagu decided to mark the final exploit of his gallant foe by placing two great boulders to mark the take-off and landing spots of the leap. The rocks are still there, standing beside the A697 in a small enclosure separated from the surrounding moorland by a stone wall and sheltered by trees.

The problem is that the two rocks are more than 30 feet apart. A leap of that size is pretty good going for any horse, never mind one carrying a man in full armour and hemmed in by the the surging, struggling mass of a mediaeval battle being fought hand-to-hand. It is true that mediaeval war horses were heavily muscled beasts, which were superbly trained for battle conditions in a way that no horse is today. Even so, this seems an almost supernaturally huge leap. However, on the other hand, Percy's Leap was famous in its day and was recognised by all as something very special.

The mystery is intensified by what happened 30 years later. By that date the Wars of the Roses were over and it was politically safe to acknowledge relatives who had died on the wrong side. Sir Ralph's brother, by then Earl of Northumberland, decided to erect a stone cross to mark the spot where his dashing younger brother had died. He spoke to survivors of the battle to make sure he had the correct place and then erected an elaborately carved cross, complete with the arms of Sir Ralph and religious scenes. The cross is still there, but it stands some 400 yards south of the boulders placed by Montagu and on the south side of the stream from where the battle began. This makes the cross not only some distance from where the leap apparently took place, but also away from the battlefield itself.

Both Montagu and Northumberland were alive at the time of the battle and should be trusted to know a great deal more about what happened there than we do today. However, the mystery remains as to whether Sir Ralph actually did perform his great leap, and why the stone cross marking his death is placed so far from the boulders. Some historians have sought to cast doubt on the entire episode. They claim that the boulders and the cross cannot both be in the right place and prefer to believe the location of the cross. They state that the leap never actually happened and that the boulders are merely natural features with no connection to the battle.

This is not necessarily the case. Sir Ralph Percy may have been pulled to the ground and speared as he landed from his leap, but he need not have died there. It can take a surprisingly long time for a fit, active man to die from even the worst wounds. There may have been plenty of time for the wounded Percy to be carried to Montagu's doctors in order to be made as comfortable as possible until he died. The doctors would have set up their makeshift hospital behind the original position of Montagu's men, which would have been south of the stream.

Perhaps that is the solution to the mystery of Percy's Leap.

The fatal Percy's Leap, which led to the death of one of the most dashing members of the Percy family, is supposed to have taken place between these two rocks on the battlefield of Hedgeley Moor.

More than a century after Sir Ralph Percy made his great leap, another feat of horsemanship won fame for a very different sort of a character, Jack of the Syde. A contemporary rhyme ran:

'A greater thief never did ride

Than Jack of the Syde.'

This Jack of the Syde was a notorious mosstrooper, a man who lived high up in the Cheviots acknowledging no law and no master and plundering both sides of the border as opportunity offered. He earned fame outside of Northumberland in 1569 when he met the fugitive Earl of Westmoreland as that rebellious nobleman was trying to escape over the border to Scotland. Instead of taking the earl and handing him over to Queen Elizabeth I for the reward money, Jack decided to help him by exchanging clothes. While Jack's men guided the earl over the border, he himself led the royal troopers a merry chase over the Cheviots.

The act made Jack the target of a royal manhunt such as he had never faced before. In 1571 he was captured and taken to Newcastle for trial and execution. He was locked up in the old keep of the castle to await his fate. His men were not content to let things rest and travelled to the city disguised as farmboys and corn hauliers. By means that are not entirely clear, the men got Jack of the Syde out of the castle the night before his execution and put him on the finest horse they could steal.

The stone cross, which tradition states marks the spot where Sir Ralph Percy died after the Battle of Hedgeley Moor.

The Tyne at Chollerford, where the bandit known as Jack of the Syde managed to escape the forces of law and order by means that remain mysterious to this day.

As dawn broke, Jack of the Syde was galloping west toward his beloved hills, but the forces of law and order were hard on his heels led by the serjeant of the watch. They were confident that they would catch him as the River Tyne was flooded and all the bridges were watched and guarded. The pursuers picked up news of Jack as they rode and learned that they were gaining on him as he headed toward Chollerton.

Riding hard, the serjeant and his men came thundering down the road to the ford. They found it frothing and boiling with a turbulent flood, the river so high that it was sweeping entire trees downstream with it. The serjeant pulled his horse to a stop. Nobody could cross the Tyne. He began to give his men instructions to spread out and search the surrounding fields and woods for Jack of the Syde.

It was then that a shout echoed over the water. There was Jack of the Syde on the far side of the Tyne, waving gleefully. How and where he had managed to get himself and his horse over the river was a mystery that was never solved. One contemporary account says this feat was performed at Chollerton Ford, another puts it a mile away at Chollerford.

In a similar vein to Jack of the Syde was the man remembered by the little town of Rothbury. This man was a notorious local mosstrooper by the name of Selby. He is generally held to have been a particularly bloodthirsty and vicious example of the type. He lived in a cave, still called Selby's Cove, high on the slopes of the Simonside Hills to the south of the town. Unfortunately, other than his name, hideout and reputation, virtually nothing is known of the man. When he lived, how he died and even his full name are entire mysteries.

When peace came to the border with the accession of King James VI of Scotland to become King James I of England, Scotland and Ireland, the violence slowly came to a close. However, not all mystery vanished from Northumberland. There is, for instance, a most peculiar grave in the churchyard at Bellingham. The tomb takes the form of a long, rounded stone lying flat on the ground and covered in mosses and lichens. It is known as the Long Pack, and in the right conditions it can almost seem to move.

The tale behind the Long Pack begins in the autumn of 1723, when Colonel Ridley of Lee Hall took his family south to London for the winter, as was his habit. Ridley had made a fortune in India serving with the East India Company and was living out a comfortable retirement surrounded by his family and wealth. He left at Lee Hall his plate and much treasure, together with three servants: Alice the housekeeper, Richard, an old houseman and Edward, a young estate worker.

One chill winter's afternoon a pedlar called at Lee Hall. In those days pedlars were welcome guests, as they not only brought useful objects to be purchased, but also carried news and gossip around the countryside. As was traditional, Alice invited the pedlar into the kitchen for a drink and something to eat. The pedlar gratefully dumped his rather huge,

The mysterious tomb known as the Long Pack in Bellingham churchyard. A strange tale of violence and revenge lies behind the enigmatic grave.

long pack on the kitchen floor and settled down to gossip about local families. He pulled out a few trinkets from his pack for Alice to inspect and she bought a couple of pieces. However, when the charming pedlar asked if he could stay the night in Lee Hall Alice refused and told him he had to go into Bellingham to find lodgings. The pedlar wheedled, but getting nowhere agreed to move on. He asked if he could leave his long pack behind as it was so heavy and promised to pick it up in the morning: Alice agreed.

When the pedlar had left, Edward and Richard came home from their duties and the three servants busied themselves about the house. Alice was alone in the kitchen preparing supper when she thought she saw the long pack move. She screamed out loud in shock, bringing the two men running. While Richard calmed Alice down, young Edward went over to the long pack and gave it a hefty kick. Nothing happened, but Alice insisted that she had seen it move. Once again Edward kicked the long pack and again nothing happened. The two men told Alice she must have imagined it, but she insisted that she had not and refused to stay in the kitchen alone. The two men had jobs to do, but did not want their supper delayed, so Edward picked up the old shotgun he used to scare away birds and fired it into the long pack. The pack twitched convulsively and blood poured out.

The two men hurriedly ripped the long pack open to find a mortally wounded man, complete with a musket, sword and a whistle. Immediately guessing that the man's whistle was to summon his comrades, the servants began barricading the windows and doors. They were only just in time for a gang of men appeared out of the darkness and began to rush the house. A furious gun battle ensued, the noise of which brought the men from nearby farms hurrying to the rescue. The gang fled, but left behind the man in the long pack. He appeared to be their leader, and as he lay dying the man volubly cursed the name of Colonel Ridley and demanded revenge for what Ridley had done in India many years earlier.

Ridley was hurriedly summoned back from London, but declared that he did not recognise the man nor could he recall any incident in India that might explain the attack. Whether he was telling the truth or not is another matter. Clearly, the man who organised the attack thought that he had reason enough to hire a gang of cut-throats and plan the assault.

As with so many other incidents and events from Northumberland's past, the affair of the long pack remains a mystery.

CHAPTER 5

MYSTERIOUS GHOSTS

Northumberland is without doubt one of the most haunted counties in England. It can seem that almost everywhere a visitor travels there is some local phantom or spook to stalk the unwary in hours of darkness. Some of these ghosts are remarkably active – the ghost at the Lord Crewe Arms in Blanchland is a case in point – others are seen less often and a few do not seem to have put in an appearance for some years, such as the Alwinton monk.

One ghost that is certainly active is the ghost at the Schooner Hotel in Alnmouth. This lovely old inn won the title of Most Haunted Hotel in Britain for the year 2002 and has featured on television and radio programmes. The manager organises regular 'Ghost Nights', which offer intrepid visitors the chance to stay overnight in the most haunted parts of the hotel. One of these is room 17, where a few guests have had an unpleasant experience, rather as if somebody with strong hands were holding them down by their

The Schooner Hotel in Alnmouth is said to be one of the most haunted hotels in England. It has featured on television and radio programmes, some of which have caught mysterious happenings live on air.

A jolly spook advertises one of many events with a supernatural theme that are held at the Schooner Hotel in Alnmouth.

throat. Fortunately, the sensation has passed off within seconds. Room 30 is also said to be haunted, though this phantom is rather more gentle and simply walks around the room, all the while remaining invisible. There is also said to be the spectre of an RAF officer walking the corridors, apparently in search of somebody to play cards with him.

The Schooner Hotel dates back to around 1660 when Alnmouth was a busy port serving farms and towns up the Aln valley and beyond. In 1806 a mighty storm altered the course of the river, making the estuary a far less secure anchorage and so reducing the importance of the town as a port. The hotel is said to have been used by smugglers and a cave where they used to store their illegal imports is said to lie behind a hidden door in the cellars. If such a room does exist, it has never been found. The ghost called Jonathan, who appears to date from the days of smugglers, is believed to have killed a man here,

The gatehouse of Bamburgh Castle, behind which lurk a number of phantoms including the mournful pink lady.

though opinions differ as to whether the quarrel was over a debt or if the victim was intending to betray the smugglers to the forces of law and order.

The moors of Alwinton had a rather more disturbing phantom. This apparition took the form of a monk wearing a dark robe and cowl who would pace slowly along the footpaths over the moors. What made the spectre so unnerving was that if it approached anybody the ghost would reach out as if imploring pity, but would reveal only the stumps of arms, with the hands appearing to have been sliced off. Cutting off a hand was punishment for theft in the Middle Ages, but one that was imposed only on persistent offenders or those guilty of outstanding crimes. How a monk could be guilty of a crime that led to both his hands being cut off is puzzling. This particular ghost was last seen in 1967 and does not seem to have walked at all in the past 40 years.

Bamburgh Castle has a number of different ghosts and must rank as one of the most haunted buildings in the county. Foremost are two phantom ladies: the pink lady and the green lady. The pink lady once lived in the royal residence that stood where the keep is now, back in the days when Bamburgh was home to the kings of Northumbria. The girl fell in love with a young knight who, for reasons unknown, did not measure up to the expectations of the girl's royal father. The king banished the young man for seven years, but the young lovers vowed to wait for each other. As the years passed, the young woman refused all of the suitors chosen for her by her father. In a rage, the king told his daughter that her absent lover had forgotten her and had married another woman. It was not true, of course, but the girl believed him. She dressed herself in the fine pink gown that she had intended to wear as a wedding dress and threw herself off the top of the tower.

She is supposed to walk through the oldest part of the castle, down to the gardens and out to the beach to look for her lover's ship. She has been seen quite often and is said to be very beautiful.

The green lady is seen standing on a crag near to the clock tower. She is dressed in a long green cloak and cradles in her arms a bundle that some have taken to be a baby. The ghost then starts off down the treacherous path that leads down to the beach. After a few steps, she seems to stumble and then to fall headlong down the cliff toward the rocks far below. Several people who have seen this ghost have taken her for a real person and have raised the alarm thinking that some unwary tourist has had an accident.

Bamburgh Castle's spectral green lady emerges from a postern gate and then takes an apparently fatal tumble down the slopes of the rock on which the castle stands.

The ghost seen in the village of Barrasford appears along this stretch of road outside the Barrasford Arms Hotel.

Among the less well-known ghosts of the castle are a man wearing a soldier's uniform of the 18th century with red coat, black hat and gold braiding. There are also the sounds of a piano being played, the voices of men and women talking quietly in a locked and empty room and the sounds of horses being ridden into the courtyard late at night. There is also a man in armour who is said to be Lord Mowbray. He was very active in the early 20th century as he clanked around the battlements, but has not been seen recently.

The ghost seen in the village of Barrasford does not have a name, but there is no real mystery as to how the haunting began. The village high street is dominated by the Barrasford Arms Hotel. This is a Victorian pub, built on the site of an ancient coaching inn, which catered to the stagecoaches running between the various towns of the north. In the 1890s the old inn caught fire and the flames raced through the building with alarming speed. One guest was seen banging on his bedroom window as the smoke billowed. Eventually, the man managed to smash the window and leapt down with his nightshirt ablaze around him. He died of his wounds a day later. Nobody knew who he was as any personal items that could have given his identity were lost in the blaze. The body was buried in an unmarked grave and the locals waited for enquiries to be made that would reveal the unfortunate man's name. However, no enquiries were ever made and the grave remains unmarked.

It is the phantom of this man which appears in the road outside the hotel from time to time. He runs screaming from one side of the road to the other, presumably recreating the terror-stricken moments as he fled the burning hotel.

Just outside Barrasford stands Haughton Castle, one of the oldest inhabited castles in England. The ghost here dates back to 1520, a time when border raids and the exactions by the reivers were at their worst. Among the most powerful clans of raiders were the Armstrongs of Liddesdale, who were frequent harriers of Northumberland.

At this time Haughton was owned by Sir Thomas Swinburne. When he heard that Cardinal Wolsey, Lord Chancellor of England, was paying a visit to York, Swinburne decided to lead a delegation of local gentry to ask Wolsey to provide more men and money to protect the border. The day before he was due to set off, Swinburne received news that a band of reivers were on his land. He hurriedly mustered a force of local men and rode off in pursuit. They caught up with the stragglers, killing two and capturing one. It was not until he had his prisoner back at Haughton that Swinburne recognised the prisoner as Archie Armstrong, one of the leading members of the Armstrong clan. Delighted, Swinburne flung Armstrong into the dungeon and then set off for York.

Haughton Castle is reputed to play host to the unpleasant phantom of Archie Armstrong of Liddesdale, one of the most ruthless reiver lords of the 16th century.

The journey south took three days, but at last Swinburne and his companions reached York and made arrangements to meet with Wolsey. Knowing that they would be staying several days in the city, the men found lodgings and began to unpack. It was while unpacking that Swinburne found he had brought with him the only key to the dungeon. Telling his companions to start without him, Swinburne leapt back on his horse and spurred north. He arrived too late. By the time the dungeon door was unlocked, Archie Armstrong was dead.

Ever since then the spirit of the forgotten reiver has stalked Haughton Castle. The ghost screams out his agonies of hunger and thirst and is a rather unsettling phantom to encounter.

Another ghost that was best avoided was the white lady of Belsay Castle. This phantom delighted in lurking by the roadsides around the village and stepping out suddenly to

The white lady of Belsay Castle is probably best avoided by anyone riding a horse, though drivers of motor vehicles seem to be immune to her dangerous stunts.

The Lord Crewe Arms at Blanchland has one of the most active ghosts in the county. The building was formerly the abbot's house of Blanchland Abbey, but the ghost dates back only to the year 1715.

frighten horses. Many a coach was sent careering dangerously off at high speed after the white lady provoked the horse team into bolting. The ghost was also able to halt plough teams in their tracks, stopping the vital work of ploughing for hours at a time. Fortunately, this white lady seems unable to affect the internal combustion engine so has been reduced to merely appearing in recent months and has not caused any real damage for years.

One of the most regularly haunted hotels in Northumberland is the Lord Crewe Arms at Blanchland. Most of the village is built upon the ruins of the old Blanchland Abbey, which was founded in 1165 and was one of the more prosperous and holy of Northumbria's monasteries. The monastery was dissolved in 1539 and the estates sold off. In 1623 the former monastery and its lands were bought by the Forsters of Bamburgh. At that time what had been the abbot's house, the adjoining guest's house and the monastic kitchen had all been combined to form a splendid manor house.

In 1715 a meeting took place here that was to have far-reaching effects. News had come from France that James Edward Stuart, eldest son of King James II, was preparing to invade Britain. James II had been ousted from his throne in 1688, after falling out with most of his subjects over the issues of Catholicism and demonstrating himself to be an outstandingly inept king and tactless man. The throne had passed to James's Protestant

The portrait of Dorothy Forster that hangs in the Lord Crewe Arms at Blanchland. It is the phantom of this lady who is said to walk the hotel with startling frequency.

daughters, Mary, and then Anne, but both had died without having children and so, in 1714, Parliament had acclaimed a cousin, George of Hanover, King George I. This move did not please many in Britain – especially the Catholics – who had been expecting James Edward to be named king.

The meeting at Blanchland was organised by young Thomas Forster and was attended by many Catholic gentlemen from across northern England. For hours they debated about how to react to the news. Most decided to wait and see what happened before committing themselves, but Thomas Forster and a few like-minded colleagues decided to declare for James Edward as soon as they heard the prince had landed in Scotland.

On 6 September the exiled prince arrived on Scottish soil where he was met by the Earl of Mar with a sizeable army at his back. Mar sent word to Forster, urging him to raise northern England in rebellion and meet the Scottish rebels at Preston. Forster sprang into action. He sent out messengers to summon the North to arms, mustered his most dependable allies and marched on Newcastle. Arriving outside the city, Forster demanded that Newcastle open its gates and declare for 'King James III', as James Edward was calling himself. The Mayor of Newcastle ordered the ramparts to be manned, and shouted down to Forster that he was a traitor. Forster loudly denounced the folk of Newcastle to be 'Georgies', or 'Geordies', for their loyalty to King George, and so gave them the name by which they have been known ever since.

Forster led the 1,000 men who had rallied to his cause to Preston. There he met 2,000 men sent south by Mar. On 13 November an army loyal to King George arrived and laid siege to Preston. At first the fighting was fierce, but seeing that his forces were heavily outnumbered, Forster soon surrendered, only to learn that Mar had already been defeated in Scotland.

Forster was taken to London to stand trial for treason. Two days before he was due in court Forster escaped. The break had been organised by his sister, Dorothy Forster, with the help of the Blanchland blacksmith. While Thomas Forster fled into exile to find James Edward, Dorothy Forster returned to the manor in Blanchland. She subsequently married a local landowner and lived out her days in happiness.

Since her death, however, Dorothy has returned to her old home in spectral form. She has been seen numerous times by staff and guests, walking quietly through the rooms of the hotel. She must feel quite at home, for the place has not changed much since she lived here. There is even a portrait of her in one of the function rooms.

The ghost of Dorothy Forster is seen most often in this small room at the Lord Crewe Arms in Blanchland.

Meanwhile, the old abbey church that stands next door to the hotel is haunted by a monk with red hair. There is no story is attached to him, which is a shame as he is seen quite often.

Another phantom clergyman haunts Callaly Castle. The haunting began when workmen were converting the old castle into modern flats. They found a small room inside the roof space that had been sealed up. When the room was broken into, it was found to be

The small village of Capheaton, where a phantom piper warns inhabitants of approaching danger.

completely empty – or so it seemed. Something must have been in there, however, for since then a ghost dubbed 'the wicked priest' has been seen and heard about the building.

At Capheaton an altogether more useful ghost takes the form of a phantom piper who warns of danger. He traditionally sounded the alert when Scottish raiders were near, but was also heard just before a fire swept through the village in 1783. He most recently manifested one night in 1940 as a vast formation of German bombers thundered overhead on their way to bomb Glasgow.

Another phantom reminder of the old border wars can be seen staggering around the boggy moors, just south of the parking area and snack bar at Carter Bar, where the A68 crosses over the Cheviots into Scotland. On 7 June 1575 the representatives of the English and Scottish monarchs met here on one of their regular appointments to dispense cross border justice and to discuss such matters as the repatriation of wanted men and compensation due to border incursions. This particular meeting went badly wrong and both sides resorted to violence. The skirmish was won by the Scots when reinforcements arrived and the English were sent south in confusion.

One of the Englishmen, Thomas Ellesden, fell victim to a sweeping blow from a massive Scottish claymore which sliced off his head. It is his ghost who is seen from time to time blundering about the moorland. The bloodshed was the last to take place between the two kingdoms, which probably accounts for its fame and the popularity of the Scottish ballad *Raid o' the Reidswire*, which tells the tale of the day.

The lonely stretch of moorland at Carter Bar where, in 1575, the unfortunate Thomas Ellesden became the last Englishman to die in the Anglo-Scottish wars. His ghost has been seen here many times.

Not far south of Carter Bar is the Catcleugh Reservoir, the shores of which are the haunt of the ghost of Percy Reed. Reed was a landowner who farmed at Troughend in the 15th century. He was a bold fighter and an honest man, so he was appointed to be a warden of the border. In this role he brought to the justice of the hangman's noose several brutal reivers of the Crosier clan. The Crosiers were determined to kill Reed and bribed Reed's neighbours, the Hall brothers, into helping them.

The fields around Troughend are the haunt of the ghost of Percy Reed, a landowner who farmed here in the 15th century and who fell victim to a savage feud.

One fatal day the Hall brothers invited Percy Reed out hunting with them and led him into an ambush laid by the Crosiers. The reivers showed no mercy and hacked Reed to pieces so thoroughly that when his grieving family came to collect the body they had to use pillowslips to pick up the pieces. Thereafter, the Halls were condemned and shunned by local folk.

Reed's ghost was soon seen striding over the moors near his old home of Troughend and down in the valley where the reservoir now stands. The ghost might be seen in his favourite green hunting coat, sounding his horn and using his whip to lay on his hounds. More often, however, he is dressed as a gentleman at home. It is said that the ghost of Reed delights in leading lost travellers back to the right road and is considered to be a very friendly phantom.

Reputedly the most haunted castle in England, Chillingham Castle is the home of perhaps the most famous ghost in Northumberland: the radiant boy. This young lad,

The gatehouse to Chillingham Castle, which is best known in supernatural circles for being home to the radiant boy, though the white lady appears to be a more active phantom at the castle.

dressed in a blue suit, haunts the pink room, usually late at night. The ghost is said to emit a weird, unearthly light as it manifests itself. Once the ghost is fully visible it utters a blood-curdling scream of terror before vanishing. In the 19th century some bones thought to belong to a child of about 10 were found under the floor of the chamber. They were given a decent burial and the frequency of the ghost's manifestations declined markedly.

Chillingham Castle has been owned by various branches of the Grey family, whose most senior members have been the earls of Tankerville since 1409, and most of the other phantoms in the castle are linked to that family. Perhaps the most active is the ghost of Lady Mary Berkeley who lived here in the 1680s. Her husband deserted her for her own sister, leaving her alone in the castle. In the years that followed, poor Lady Mary paced the corridors distraught and forlorn. She walks them still. Guides at the castle have reported that the sounds of a lady's high heels accompanied by the rustle of a heavy silk dress are heard almost weekly.

Another phantom woman at Chillingham is the white lady, who haunts the kitchens and domestic quarters. The mutter of male voices deep in conversation is sometimes heard in the library. Although words cannot be made out there are two distinct tones of voice, and one guide once timed the conversation as lasting for 18 seconds.

An odd story from Chillingham dates back to the 1750s when work was being carried out to convert the grim old border fortress into a comfortable modern residence. Workmen were stripping a wall of plaster when they found a blocked up doorway. Breaking the stonework down, they found a small chamber, in the middle of which stood a large wooden

The land around the beach at Cresswell is haunted by a white lady who died after a tragic love affair around 1,000 years ago.

chair upon which sat a skeleton wearing the clothes of a gentleman from the Tudor times. The clothes crumbled to dust as soon as they were touched, as did the bones.

A lady in white haunts the land between the old pele tower of Cresswell and the beach. According to an old story recorded in the 19th century, the ghost is that of a Saxon maiden who fell in love with a Viking trader some time in the 10th century. This was a dangerous time for romances across the community divide, for many Vikings preferred raiding to trading and the English were understandably nervous about visitors from overseas.

Tragedy struck one day when the Viking trader came to visit his beloved. She was the daughter of the family who then lived in the pele tower that forms the heart of Cresswell Castle, and so was up on a turret watching out for her lover's ship to come within sight. Unfortunately, a gang of local men saw the ship first and took it to be a raider. As the Norseman waded ashore, he was set upon and killed before he could explain himself. The unfortunate young woman promptly went mad and spent the rest of her short life wandering the village and shore, searching for the man she was convinced would one day return to her.

Another lady ghost haunts Denton Hall, though she seems to be quite a different sort of phantom. This ghost takes the form of an elderly woman dressed in the fashions of the 18th century. She has been recorded since at least the 1840s and wanders the house at dusk, as if checking that all is in order before the family retires for the night. She is said to have the remarkable habit of appearing to a person only once. The successive owners of the house have each seen her shortly after moving in, but have not been bothered thereafter. Guests and visitors, on the other hand, report her with consistent frequency.

An altogether sadder phantom lady haunts Dilston Castle. In 1715 this was the home of James Radcliffe, the Earl of Derwentwater, one of the leading Catholic noblemen of England. When the news arrived that the Catholic heir to the ousted King James II had landed in Scotland, messages ran around northern England urging Catholics to rise in rebellion against the Protestant King George I. Derwentwater received a persuasive letter from his friend, Thomas Forster of Blanchland, and decided to ride with the rebels.

As Derwentwater led his troop of 30 cavalrymen out of Dilston, he glanced around at his ancestral lands and, perhaps for the first time, realised that he was gambling not only his own life, but also the inheritance of his son, on an uncertain uprising. He drew rein, sat in thought for a while and then turned back for home. As he pulled up in the courtyard, the young earl was struck on the head by a fan hurled from an upstairs window by his furious wife.

'Take that,' she shouted, 'and give your sword to me.'

James Radcliffe, the Earl of Derwentwater, was executed in London in 1715 and his body brought back to Dilston Chapel for burial. His ghost now haunts the surrounding area.

Shamed by his wife, Derwentwater rode off to war. The rebellion failed and the young earl was taken to London for trial and inevitable execution. On the day he was beheaded at the Tower of London, 24 February 1716, the stream that runs around Dilston ran red as if it were blood and the corn milled on the estate came out crimson. The earl's body was at first buried in London, but was later brought back to Dilston and interred inside the little chapel beside the castle.

Lady Derwentwater was widely blamed for her husband's death and was shunned by the locals, who had loved the earl and regarded him as a caring landlord. She died in 1723 at the age of only 30, having wasted away and fallen prey to smallpox. Within days her ghost was seen wandering through the castle and the grounds, while the ghost of her husband was seen down by the stream. A ditty came to be sung by local children that runs:

'The Countess wails in Dilston Hall

But Radcliffe is not there.'

The titles and estates passed to James's younger brother, Charles. He joined the uprising of 1745 that aimed to put James Edward's son, Bonnie Prince Charlie, on the throne. That uprising did rather better than that of 1715, but it too ended in failure. Charles was executed on the same spot as his brother on 8 December 1746. The estates were confiscated by the crown and handed over to Greenwich Hospital to provide income to care for wounded sailors.

Much larger and more imposing than Dilston is Dunstanburgh Castle, which stands on a rocky headland overlooking the North Sea. The steep-sided rocky outcrop has been inhabited off and on since the Bronze Age, but the present castle was built in the 1300s by Thomas, Earl of Lancaster. This powerful nobleman ruled much of northern England on behalf of King Edward I and erected Dunstanburgh Castle to be the administrative headquarters for handing out justice and collecting taxes, as well as a bulwark against any Scottish invasion.

When Edward died and his son, Edward II, came to the throne Lancaster fell out of royal favour. Lancaster was a tough warrior, brought up to live in the saddle and fight the Scots, while Edward preferred soft silks, rich meals and the arms of his gay lover, Piers Gaveston. It was not surprising that the two men fell out. In addition, unfortunately, Gaveston had a wicked tongue and cruel wit that he seemed unable to control. The butt of many of his jokes was Lancaster, who lacked the social graces that Edward admired. In 1308 Edward gave Gaveston a high office, but the good-looking knight bungled the task and was voted into exile by the nobles. Edward then brought him back, but Gaveston proved to be as incompetent as before. This time Lancaster would not settle for exile and instead had Gaveston murdered. He then made himself guardian of England. Edward overthrew Lancaster's rule in 1321, and when Lancaster tried to raise an armed rebellion Edward had him executed. The execution was bungled, with the axeman taking no less than nine strokes to separate the earl's head from his shoulders.

The ghost of Thomas wanders the ruins of Dunstanburgh, and a truly terrifying apparition he is too. The ghost appears with the mangled head lolling sideways from a half-severed neck, the blood and gore terrible to see.

Dunstanburgh Castle was built in the 1300s by Thomas, Earl of Lancaster, who still haunts the fortress that he founded so many years ago.

Altogether less disturbing is the other phantom of Dunstanburgh. This ghost comes in the shape of an elegant lady strolling slowly around the area of the keep. She is identified as the ghost of Margaret of Anjou, queen to King Henry VI. It was Henry's intermittent insanity and Margaret's corrupt rule that plunged England into the Wars of the Roses, as a coalition of noblemen and gentry sought to wrest power and hand it over to the less dishonest and more business-friendly hands of the York dynasty.

The civil war went badly for Margaret and finally she was reduced to holding only a few fortresses in the north, of which Dunstanburgh was one and Bamburgh another. Henry was pathetically paraded around by Margaret in his kingly robes, but nobody took him seriously any longer. Eventually the pair were captured by the new Yorkist monarch, Edward IV. Henry died a suspiciously convenient death soon after, while Margaret endured four years in prison before she was ransomed by her relative, King Louis XI of France. She died in 1482 in France, but her ghost walks here in Dunstanburgh where she spent her final months of freedom, hoping for victory that could never be hers.

Most ghosts are not of exalted persons, such as the earl of Lancaster or the queen of England, and a few are entirely nameless. The ghostly man of Ellingham, for instance, is widely known, but nobody has any idea who he is. The phantom has been seen many times running down the high street of the village chasing a phantom horse which has trailing reins. It is believed that the horse threw the man – but why the scene should be recreated in ghostly fashion is a mystery.

The name of the ghost that haunts Winter's Gibbet on the moors above Elsdon is known. It is William Winter, from whom the place takes its name. William Winter was hanged on 11 August 1792 for the murder of Margaret Crosier, who lived in Haws Pele. The murder had been carried out one year earlier by Winter and two cousins, Jane and Eleanor Park, who all belonged to a group of gypsies known as the Faws. Elderly Margaret Crosier owned a shop which catered to the drovers who urged their herds down the road over the lonely moors to take advantage of the grazing they offered. The Park sisters had visited her shop some months earlier and had become convinced that the old woman kept a good sum of money in the house. They recruited Winter to help them rob the house, but Winter had got carried away and had murdered the old woman when she had refused to tell him where her money was hidden.

Crosier was caught when a local shepherd boy spotted a boot mark near the scene of the crime with an unusual pattern of hobnails in it. He recalled seeing a burly traveller two days earlier with identical boots and was able to give the magistrate a detailed description. This led to the arrest of Winter, who had some stolen items in his possession, and that led to the arrest of his known associates. All three were hanged, but only Winter's body

The Winter's Gibbet stands high on the moors above Elsdon and is haunted by the ghost of the man hanged here in 1792: William Winter.

was brought here to be hung in chains as a grisly warning to any other travellers who felt tempted to commit murder to gain riches.

The ghost of Winter has been seen walking around the gibbet and moving toward the wood where his bones were buried in a rough hole after his flesh had rotted away. The gibbet has been replaced more than once since, with the grisly body of Winter being represented by a wooden effigy – only the head of which remained in 2009.

It is the murder victim, not the murderer, who haunts Featherstone Castle – and there is not just one of them. The first is Sir Reginald FitzUrse, a local landowner who fell foul of the owner of Featherstone Castle back in the 13th century. Clearly a rather unpleasant chap, the owner not only chained Sir Reginald in the dungeon, but proceeded to starve him to death by inches. Each day the unhappy prisoner was given a tiny amount of food – not enough to live on but just enough to give him hope.

There was no hope, of course, and Sir Reginald died an agonising death. Ever since then his phantom has stalked the older parts of the castle. When he feels in the mood, the phantom clanks his chains and moans horribly.

The second phantom – or rather, host of phantoms – dates back to the 15th century when Abigail, daughter of Lord Featherstone, fell in love with the son and heir of the nearby Ridley family. Unfortunately the Ridleys and Featherstones were on bad terms

Featherstone Castle is haunted by an entire procession of ghosts; the doleful reminder of a wedding feast that went horribly wrong.

and Abigail's father disapproved of the match. He banned young Ridley from visiting and lined up a man he deemed to be more suitable for his daughter.

The wedding took place the following year at Featherstone Castle amid great festivities. As the feast went on, the groom suggested that he and his bride should lead a walk of the guests around the estate and to the nearby villages to display the wealth and finery of the occasion to the locals. The guests applauded the idea and quickly lined up to be led out. Lord Featherstone, however, was too busy drinking with his cronies and declined to go.

Some hours later night fell and Lord Featherstone began to get worried. His guests had intended to be gone for only a couple of hours. Riders were sent out to summon them back to the hall for the evening's entertainment. Then, as midnight struck, the castle gates opened to admit the returning procession led by the bride and groom. However, something was terribly wrong. The procession made no sound as it moved. The boots and shoes clumped down noiselessly, the jewellery glittered but did not tinkle and the merry chatter was stilled. For this procession was not the same one that had left, but was instead the phantom return of the guests – and each ghost bore the marks of the fatal wounds and blows that it had suffered.

The appalled Lord Featherstone watched in horror as the gruesome procession entered the feasting hall and then faded from sight. A messenger then rode in to say that he had found the bodies of the slaughtered procession in Pinkeyn Clough, a wooded ravine on the estate. The Ridleys had been to blame.

The ghostly procession is still seen from time to time, though more often it is only the sorrowing Abigail who walks in phantom form around the gardens and down to Pinkeyn Clough.

The monument that marks the site of the Battle of Flodden Field. King James IV of Scotland was killed here, along with most of his nobility and soldiers. The ghosts of the battlefield seem to mourn the dead.

Slaughter on an even larger scale led to the haunting of Flodden Field, just outside the village of Branxton. In the summer of 1513 King James IV of Scotland invaded England, which was then at war with France, and offered a tempting target. By a fatal combination of timid strategy and rash tactics, King James managed to get himself and most of his army trapped against the foot of a steep hill, the main English army to his front and a substantial English force to his rear. There could be no escape for the Scots. Over 10,000 of the invaders were killed that day, including King James, plus numerous earls, knights and gentry. It was said that every family in Scotland had at least one member slain on Flodden Field.

It is no wonder then that ghostly men in armour have been seen on the battlefield. Some say that the spectres recreate the bloody fighting, hacking at each other with phantom weapons. Other witnesses say that the ghosts simply stand staring about themselves while exuding a sad and melancholy aura.

Similar phantoms prowl the battlefield of Otterburn. This battle took place in 1388 and within months had become the most famous in Europe as minstrels sang of it from one end of Christendom to the other. The reason behind the battle's fame lay not its importance in the ongoing conflicts between England and Scotland, but was due to the almost chivalric nature of the contest.

The campaign began in July when a large Scottish force under Sir James Douglas, the most famous knight in Scotland, poured over the border to pillage and loot as much of northern England as they could before an English army could be mustered to face them. The Scots got as far as Newcastle before they were faced with a sizeable English force

The haunted battlefield of Otterburn, seen from what was the centre of the Scottish position. The flanking charge led by Douglas came down this slope from left to right to defeat the English army.

under Sir Henry Percy, known as Harry Hotspur for his gallantry and skill in both battle and tournament. The English force was not large enough to face the Scots in open battle, but reinforcements were expected so Hotspur decided to sally out in an effort to goad the Scots into staying outside Newcastle, rather than taking the more prudent course of retreating with their loot. The sally backfired when Hotspur's standard-bearer was unhorsed and his flag snatched by a Scotsman.

While Douglas and the Scots retreated that evening, Hotspur waited impatiently for the English reinforcements to arrive. He was furious that Douglas had managed to capture his banner and vowed that the silken flag would never reach Scotland. Douglas heard about this boast when he reached Otterburn. With chivalrous courage, Douglas halted his army to allow Hotspur to catch up and make an attempt at recapturing the disputed flag.

Hotspur did not wait for the expected men to reach Newcastle, but instead set off at top speed as soon as he could persuade his fellow knights to follow him. The English caught up with the Scots just west of Otterburn on the evening of 19 August. True to his nickname, Hotspur launched an immediate attack. The battle carried on into the night and was fought by eerie moonlight. When Douglas launched a surprise flank attack, Hotspur and his men were forced back toward the River Rede. Once their formation was broken, the English fled back to the cover of Otterburn Castle to await the dawn. Hotspur was captured, but Douglas was killed.

The ghosts are said to roam the slopes between the Otter Burn and the battle monument, which was erected by a later member of the Percy Family to mark the site of Hotspur's most famous exploit and only defeat. Most historians agree that the main fighting took place on this hill and the ghosts would seem to back this theory up.

Yet another victim of a violent death haunts the road leading up to Bellister Castle outside Haltwhistle. The phantom seems to have been most active in the 19th century, though it has been encountered several times during the 20th century. The ghost takes the form of an elderly man wearing a long grey cloak and carrying a bundle or sack. He plods slowly up the road from the site of the former ferry over the Tyne. When any one approaches him, the spectre turns around to show a face hideously distorted by a savage wound.

It is said that this grey man of Bellister is the phantom of a wandering minstrel who used to ply his trade up and down the Tyne Valley during the Middle Ages. The Lord of Bellister Castle became convinced that the minstrel was really a spy in the pay of the Scots and was using his journeys to ascertain the state of defence of the various castles, pele towers and strongholds of the English. The lord had the minstrel arrested, but he broke free and ran down toward the Tyne. So the lord set his hunting hounds loose and gave chase. The dogs caught up with the unfortunate man on the river bank and tore him to pieces. Ever afterwards, his ghost haunted the lord and, after his death, the road to the castle.

The grey man of Bellister walks to the castle from the Tyne, but if he turns to look at you be prepared for a terrible shock.

The River Coquet at Hepple is home to an enigmatic but lifesaving phantom mounted on a great black horse.

Nearby Knaresdale Hall is haunted by a pretty young woman in a white dress. Both her clothing and her hair are soaking wet, which provides a clue to the background of the tale. The girl discovered that the Lady of Knaresdale was having an affair with her husband's nephew and was murdered to ensure her silence, her body weighted down and thrown into a pond. Her ghost appeared several times over the following days, causing Lady Knaresdale to first go mad and then to confess her crimes. The girl's body was retrieved and given a Christian burial, but this did nothing to calm her ghost which continues to walk to this day.

Another water-related phantom haunts Hepple, or rather the banks of the River Coquet just south of the village. He appears mounted on a great black charger and rides up and down the riverbanks, cracking his whip as if to drive any mortals away from the river. Invariably, a flood follows his appearances, so anyone who sees him is well advised to head for higher ground.

The holy island of Lindisfarne is a remarkably peaceful and tranquil spot – at least when the ghosts are not walking. The best known phantom is that of St Cuthbert himself, who is said to sit on the beach making St Cuthbert's Beads, which are pebbles with a hole through them. There is also a spectral white dog which trots around the

Lobster pots on the holy island of Lindisfarne, where the phantom of a drowned sailor pleads silently for help that can only come too late.

monastic ruins, and a lady in a white dress who is said to be Lady Constance Beverley. The saddest phantom is that of the drowned sailor who taps on the window of the former coastguard's cottage beside the ruins. Presumably he is seeking the help that never came to him.

The ghost of Howick Hall, just outside Alnwick, is at first glance a rather mundane sort of a spectre. She takes the form of an old lady in a long Victorian dress and bonnet who walks about the hall in silence. This is, however, a most unusual phantom. If anyone tries to approach her she lifts up the skirts of her dress in a very immodest and most un-Victorian fashion and then sinks slowly into the ground, her feet vanishing first and her head last.

Equally unusual, but considerably more frightening, is the ghost of ruined Mitford Castle. This alarming apparition takes the form of a knight in armour who pops into vision suddenly and usually very close to the unlucky witness. In one hand the tall knight wields a bloody sword which he brandishes with vigour, in his other is a severed head, still dripping blood and gore onto the turf. Who he was, or who his victim was, is unknown, but the severed head opens its mouth to scream and gibber. The phantom remains in sight for only a few seconds before vanishing abruptly.

The various ghosts of Newcastle upon Tyne, for centuries the largest city in the county, are generally less alarming to encounter than the ghostly knight of Mitford Castle, but they can be frightening enough when stumbled upon unexpectedly. The most haunted place in the city is the old castle keep, which still dominates the central area. Despite popular opinion, this is not the New Castle that gave the city its name, but the one built in 1172

The gaunt ruins of Mitford Castle are haunted by perhaps the most startling phantom in all Northumberland.

The towering keep of Newcastle Castle houses the saddest phantom in all the city.

to replace the original New Castle of 1080. For many centuries the castle and the city walls that surrounded it were a key part in the defence of northern England against the marauding Scots. Once the wars were over, the city walls were gradually dismantled and the castle put to other uses.

One of these uses was as the city prison and it is in this role that the most active and saddest of the castle's spectres belong. In the late 18th century a flower girl was thrown in prison for debt. One day the unfortunate flower girl found herself confronted by a brutal fellow prisoner who raped and murdered her and then stashed her body in a dark corner. The poor girl's ghost has walked the keep ever since, accompanied by the scent of flowers.

The famous tower and arched lantern of Newcastle Cathedral houses the ghost of a knight in armour, who was seen several times during the 19th century.

Rather more ominous is the black shadow that emerges from the ancient walls, moves along corridors and crosses rooms before melting back into the ancient stones from which it came.

Not far from the haunted castle is the haunted cathedral. It was built as the parish church of St Nicholas in the 14th century and was promoted to cathedral status in 1882, when the new diocese of Newcastle was formed. It is famous for its 15th-century lantern balanced on two intersecting stone arches on top of the tower, though the numerous memorials inside make it worth a visit as well.

The ghost there is that of a knight in armour who was seen several times during the 19th century, but who seems to be rather less active these days. His favourite trick was to step out from behind a pillar and then step back out of sight again.

Considerably older than any of these phantoms is the ghost that haunts the Hancock Museum. This strutting spectre is generally thought to be a ghost from ancient Egypt. It was not witnessed until a 3,000-year-old mummy case was acquired by the museum and it is usually seen walking close to where the case is displayed. Fortunately for the many visitors who throng the museum, the ghost walks only by moonlight and is therefore encountered only by museum staff.

Down on Newcastle Quayside there are a number of phantoms. The most active is the ghost of Henry Hardwick, a local fisherman who plied his trade out of Newcastle in the 1790s. At that date Britain had been fighting a decade long series of wars against France and the navy were short of men. Parliament gave the navy permission to 'press-gang' men into the navy. In theory the press gangs were supposed to force only single men without gainful employment, but some captains were desperate for men and the gangs they sent out were none too particular about whom they took. Many an honest family man was kidnapped and bundled on-board a ship which was sailing for the wars and would not return for some years.

Henry Hardwick was out one evening when he spotted a press gang coming his way up the Quayside. He made a run for it, ducking into the steep alleyway that runs up beside the Cooperage public house. What happened next is unclear, but the corpse of the unfortunate Henry Hardwick was found the next morning, lying in the alleyway with his head battered in. The press gang denied all knowledge of the crime, and since their motive was to force live men on-board ship they were believed. The crime was never solved, which may explain why the phantom Henry Hardwick patrols the alley and adjacent areas of Quayside to this day.

Not far away is the John Wesley Memorial, which was erected on the spot where the city gallows used to stand. The ghost here is that of Jane Jameson, a woman who, in 1829, murdered her mother to get her hands on the old lady's money. Jane did her best to pass

The narrow lane beside the ancient Cooperage public house is haunted by the spectre of a fisherman, who died here in suspicious circumstances more than two centuries ago.

the blame onto her boyfriend, planting some of the stolen property in his home and providing the magistrates with incriminating evidence against him. However, her efforts were to no avail and her guilt was uncovered. She was hanged here and her ghost has been seen pacing sadly around the spot, usually in the evening. She is said to cry out for her lover to come to her, but given her heartless actions that seems rather unlikely.

Newcastle's Tyne Theatre plays host to a gentle phantom, though he is still able to startle actors who encounter him.

An altogether more gentle phantom is to be found at the Tyne Theatre. This is the spectre of an actor who was killed when a heavy piece of scenery collapsed on top of him a century or so ago. He is usually seen on stage, but may also appear sitting in the stalls and watching rehearsals, which is rather unnerving for those on stage at the time.

The little hamlet of Old Hazelrigg plays host to a ghostly horseman who thunders along the lane mounted on a great charger while waving a sword above his head. This phantom is usually identified as being that of a Scottish reiver who was killed here in a savage skirmish in the 1490s.

Another phantom horseman rides near Rock Hall, just north of Alnwick. This spectre can be clearly identified from his dress as a cavalier of the 17th century and is usually said to be linked to the English Civil War, though no precise story is attached to him.

Sometimes seen walking to the hall from the village of South Charlton is a mournful female ghost. She is said to appear only on 15 August, though some witnesses claim to have seen her at other dates over the summer months. She is believed to be mourning her husband who died on that date.

An equally enigmatic female ghost haunts the Otterburn Tower Hotel, a fine mock-mediaeval mansion built in the early 19th century to incorporate the remains of the

The Otterburn Tower Hotel is haunted by a lady who walks the corridors at night.

mediaeval Otterburn Castle. The ghost here is that of a lady dressed in grey or pale blue who walks the corridors at night. She is said to be the wraith of a chambermaid who died here in 1830 at the age of just 32. There were, it seems, suspicious circumstances that pointed towards the dead woman's husband as having reasons to be rid of her, but nothing was ever proved. Perhaps the lack of a conviction for her death brings the ghost back time after time.

No such story attaches itself to the lady ghost of High Rochester. This tiny hamlet stands on the slopes above the village of Rochester and occupies the site of a small Roman fort that was built here as a forward base north of Hadrian's Wall in around AD 150. The woman is said to be linked to the Roman fortress, not to the more recent farmhouses. She appears half naked and wanders the area weeping, though nobody knows why.

Nor is it entirely clear why the grey lady of Seaton Delaval Hall should haunt the chapel of the house. She carries in her arms a baby and is generally said, though without any firm evidence, to be an early member of the Delaval family. That the ghost carries a baby to the chapel may indicate that some tragedy occurred. Perhaps both mother and child died in childbirth and the distraught mother is bringing her baby here for the christening it never received.

In the churchyard at Warden there lies the grave of an unfortunate young woman who was abandoned by her lover and subsequently died of a broken heart in the early 19th century. A few days after she died a plant grew from her grave which soon produced a bright yellow flower of great beauty and ethereal scent. Nobody could identify the flower and efforts to collect seeds failed. It marked the grave for a while and then withered and died.

The Bay Horse pub at Stamfordham closed down in 2008, though at the time the closure was intended to be only temporary. The pub was built as a fortified farmhouse in the 1560s and converted to an inn in around 1690. The most frequently reported ghost is that of a woman in the kitchen, who seems to be annoyed at those who intrude on what was presumably her domain when she was alive. There is also said to be a ghostly priest in the main dining room, but the evidence for him is not so compelling.

The land around Thirlwall Castle is said to be haunted by the 'Cauld Lad'. This boy was an orphan who had come to work at the castle, but who for some reason had fallen

The Bay Horse pub at Stamfordham has been examined by teams of paranormal investigators, who are convinced that this is the scene of a very active haunting indeed.

Thirlwall Castle is haunted by a phantom who has been nicknamed 'The Cauld Lad'. He will tell anyone who listens to him how cold he is.

foul of the lord of the place. The boy was turned out on a cold winter's night and his body was found frozen to death nearby. His unhappy ghost shivers its way around the ruined walls and surrounding lands muttering, 'I'm so cauld, so cauld, so cauld.'

The ghosts of Wallington House are even more restless. They have never been seen, but the sounds of trunks and packing cases being packed and unpacked repeatedly echoes through the house at night. There are also said to be ghostly birds here, though they have not been seen since the 1860s.

The imposing edifice of Warkworth Castle seems almost made to be haunted, but instead the ghosts frequent the riverside at the foot of the great rock on which the castle was built. The riverside path is haunted by Lady Margaret Neville, wife to the Earl of Northumberland, and mother of the Sir Henry Percy nicknamed Hotspur for his bravery in battle against the Scots.

A short distance along the River Coquet from the castle stands a cave set into the river bank that in mediaeval times was a hermitage. The first hermit to have lived here was said

Warkworth Castle seen reflected in the waters of the Coquet. The riverside path is haunted by Lady Margaret Neville, wife to the Earl of Northumberland, and mother of Sir Henry Percy, who held court here during his glory years.

to have been a knight who accidentally killed his own brother in battle against the Scots and who came here to atone for his sins with a lifetime of prayer. Whatever the truth of that tale, a ghostly monk has been seen moving swiftly about the place.

At Woodhorn, St Mary's churchyard is haunted by a local man, Tom Chalkley, who in 1914 was serving in the Royal Navy as World War One broke out. In 1916 his ship was sunk in the Battle of Jutland, a great clash between the fleets of both sides that ended in a stalemate. The unfortunate sailor's ghost was seen here on the day he died and has returned ever since. Perhaps he wishes to relive happier days at home.

Quite why a spectral skeleton riding a a bike should be seen in the lane outside the church is unclear, but the ghostly skeleton of Woodhorn could stand for all the ghosts of Northumberland. It is utterly mysterious, bizarre, unexplained and yet, it exists. The ghost goes about its business without seeming to so much as notice those that it frightens. And so the ghosts wander about Northumberland, adding their own mystery to this most mysterious of counties.

Chapter 6

Mysterious Witches

There has probably been more mystery and confusion about witches than any other subject. Who the witches were (or are), what they do and why they do it is open to almost as many interpretations and views as there are people who have studied the subject.

The key problem seems to lie in the fact that most of those who study witches have been educated people from the towns, while witches and the people they deal with have generally been from rural areas and have had little formal education. The result has been that most studies of witchcraft, or what purports to be it, have been based on a fundamental misconception of the phenomenon itself. The assorted tales of the witches of Northumberland go some way to stripping away the mistakes and confusions to allow us to get to the heart of the mystery.

The most famous witch of Northumberland is the notorious Meg of Meldon. That Meg was a real person is beyond doubt. She was born in about 1570, the daughter of William Selby, a wealthy banker of Newcastle. Selby had a reputation as being a somewhat ruthless moneylender, who insisted on prompt payment of debts and was not above hiring tough men to hand out violence to those who defaulted. Nothing illegal was ever proved against him, however, and Selby mixed with the cream of local society. As her beauty became as evident as her father's wealth, young Meg was counted to be a good catch and everyone began to wonder who would be lucky enough to get her up the aisle.

In the event, the lucky man turned out to be Sir William Fenwick of Wallington Hall. The Fenwicks were a famous fighting family, always to the fore, whether in driving off Scottish raiders, or in exacting revenge by riding over the mountains to seize cattle and loot from the Scottish lowlands. In Sir William's day, Wallington Hall was a fortified home based on a pele tower that was already some centuries old. The modern comfortable Italianate mansion was built some decades later. The marriage was widely considered to be a good one. Sir William brought a title and ancient lineage, while Meg brought wealth.

Meg's wealth took a somewhat unusual form. Her father settled on the happy young couple no actual cash, but instead the debts and mortgages on a number of properties, business and other establishments. The regular repayments on these debts provided a comfortable income for Meg and Sir William and enabled them to live in some style at Wallington Hall.

Quite when the rumours about Meg first began to circulate is unclear. Without doubt, however, the first crime for which her witchcraft was widely blamed took place in 1614. By this time Sir William had died suddenly and Meg was left with seven young children to bring up. She held the spreading Fenwick estates in trust for her eldest boy, William, heir to the deceased Sir William. But that was not enough: she wanted wealth and lands of her own.

Meg's eye fell on Meldon Hall, and the 500 acres of prime farming land that went with it. The estate was one on which she held a mortgage, that had been given to her father. Meldon Hall was the property of the Herons, a clan as old and respected as the Fenwicks. The then head of the Herons was not the cleverest with money. When raids upon Scotland had ended as a source of income, he had continued to spend freely, quickly eating up more cash than his estate could produce. The Heron's son and heir was a popular, good-looking young man who had been given a good education and was busy establishing himself as a merchant in order to provide a solid income.

Meg bided her time. She waited until the Heron heir was far away on a trading voyage, then she struck. The head of the Heron clan died a sudden and suspiciously convenient death. Meg demanded the instant repayment of the loan. This was, undoubtedly, her

The tomb of Sir William Fenwick of Wallington Hall in Meldon church. His wife would achieve lasting infamy as Meg of Meldon, the most powerful witch ever to stalk Northumberland.

right according to the loan contract, but the manner in which it was done was deeply unfair to the Heron heir. Given time, the young man would have been able to secure a new loan from a bank and so repay Meg, but she did not give him the chance. Meg foreclosed and seized Meldon Hall and its estate. In this way she gained her name of Meg of Meldon.

Not long after this event, Meg grabbed Hartington Hall when that owner also failed to stick to an obscure clause in his loan. Again it was widely rumoured that Meg had used witchcraft to get her hands on the estate. It was soon said that Meg had magically created an underground passage that linked Meldon to Hartington. It was said she was in the habit of flitting at supernatural speed along the tunnel to pass secretly between her two ill-gotten mansions. While the Hartington and Meldon estates prospered, those of her neighbours did not produce such profitable crops. Once again the locals muttered that Meg of Meldon was using witchcraft.

The rumours persisted until Meg's death, but nothing had ever been proved so she was given a Christian burial at Newminster Abbey, near Morpeth. She left her property to her eldest son, William, who had long since inherited the Fenwick estates when he had turned 21. Oddly, however, no cash at all was included. Meg of Meldon had not deposited her money in any bank and there was no hoard of gold or silver coins at either Meldon or Hartington. This was peculiar as she had always paid her debts promptly in cold hard cash while she was alive.

Soon after Meg of Meldon's death a phantom black dog the size of a pony was seen patrolling Meldon village and the surrounding farmland, taking a particular interest in Meldon Bridge. Such phantom dogs are generally considered to be bad luck and a story spread rapidly around Meldon that the new arrival was Meg returned in spectral form. Then news came that Meg of Meldon was haunting Newminster graveyard, taking the form of a lady clad in a long, white, funeral shroud. Soon the phantom Meg of Meldon had left Newminster and instead was seen wandering around Meldon and Hartington accompanied by the great black dog.

Then seven years after Meg of Meldon had died, the terrifying pair had gone. The months passed and still they were not seen. Locals believed that they were free of the phantoms, but it was not to be. After a further seven years the two phantoms were back. As before, they walked at night around Meldon and Hartington, always following the same route.

Then one day the ceiling in a house that Meg of Meldon had once owned suddenly caved in and a leather bag came crashing down, breaking as it hit the floor and spilling a heap of silver coins across the floor. A quick inspection showed that the coins dated back to the time when Meg of Meldon had lived. Speculation quickly raced ahead of the

Today Meldon is a quiet little village, rather out of the way, but in the days of Meg of Meldon it was, if the stories are to be believed, at the very heart of evil in the county.

evidence until it was firmly believed that the terrible ghosts of Meg of Meldon and the black hound were keeping an eye on the places where Meg had hidden her vast treasure.

One Meldon farmer dreamt that he had met the ghost of Meg in his farmyard. The ghost told him that she had hidden an oxhide stuffed full of golden coins down the farmer's well. She instructed him to haul it out, saying that he had to distribute half the treasure to charities and good causes but that he could keep the other half for himself. In the dream the ghost imposed one condition: that the process of hauling up the gold should be completed in absolute silence. Otherwise, she warned, the devil she had worshipped would get the gold instead.

The farmer promptly found a grappling hook and iron chain, which he threw down the well until he caught the hook on something heavy. The man began to pull the weight up laboriously, hand over hand. He was finally rewarded by the appearance of a leather bag of great size at the top of the well parapet. The man made a lunge forward to grab the bag, calling out triumphantly 'Ha! Now no demon alive can stop me getting it.'

There was a sudden flash of light, the chain broke and the bag toppled back down into the well. The man cursed, but his luck was out. He had spoken before grabbing the gold and so had lost it forever.

Another witch of awesome power lived at Seaton Delaval in the 17th century. This old crone was said to have the power to blight crops, but at the same time could cure sickly crops. She could cause livestock to sicken with a glance of her eye, or cure the most deadly of cattle murrains with a wave of her hand. She was a curse and a blessing to the good folk of Seaton Delaval.

Eventually, the tales of her prowess reached the ears of the Lord of Seaton Delaval. He did not hold with witchcraft, believing it to be the work of the Devil, so he decided to pay a visit to the witch. As the lord approached the old woman's cottage, he heard the sound of chanting. Creeping forward, he peered in through the window. He saw the old woman gleefully prancing around the room, while a great black pot boiled on the fire. The woman was plucking bunches of herbs and nameless objects from shelves and tossing them into the pot. As she did so she chanted:

'This to make the young lambs swell and die,

This to blight the apple blossom,

This to make the cowherds bone ache and ache and ache'

Horror-struck at the supernatural evil being done in front of his eyes, the young lord kicked the door down, overturned the pot and grabbed the witch. He hauled her off to trial, where his account of her evil intentions, in addition to the tales told by her neighbours, were enough to have her condemned to death. Perhaps surprisingly, this did not prove to be a popular decision with the witch's neighbours. They said that some mercy should be shown, but the judge was adamant that being in league with the Devil and harming her neighbours was enough to earn death. He said that the old woman could have one final wish, but that she must hang.

The witch of Seaton Delaval asked her neighbours to bring her two wooden bowls that had never been used. From these, she said, she would eat her final meal and she gave some precise instructions as to what food she wanted. However, when the wooden dishes were brought, the witch ignored the food and instead placed one foot on each dish. She muttered a spell and rose high into the sky, cackling loudly.

'We are tricked,' called out the judge. 'She is escaping.'

'Oh no,' shouted out the man who had brought the wooden dishes. 'I thought the cunning old woman was up to no good. One of those dishes has been used before. Watch.'

As the crowd watched, the witch began to wobble in mid-air. Then one of the dishes gave way and fell, bringing the witch tumbling down with it. Both splashed into the chilly waters of the North Sea and the witch was seen no more.

The first trial for witchcraft in Northumberland was held on 23 July 1604 when Anne Nevelson and Katherine Thompson were both charged. The two women had been going about their business as local healers without much trouble, but had fallen foul of a clergyman who took exception to their use of spells and claims to be able to practise magic. Witnesses said that Nevelson and Thompson kept a white duck and a white drake. When asked to cure a sick person the women brought these birds and pressed their bills against the mouths of the patient, while muttering and mumbling spells. Found guilty, the women were fined.

Twenty-four years passed before the next witchcraft trial in Northumberland. This time it was a woman named Jane Robson from Leeplish in Tyndale who was on trial. The court records state that the main charge against her was that she had murdered her sister-in-law, Mabel Robson, also of Leeplish. The crime of witchcraft was merely a secondary charge. Unfortunately, the records for the year are incomplete and the outcome of the trial is not recorded.

The case of Dorothy Swinow in 1650 is rather better recorded. The trouble seems to have begun in 1645 when Dorothy caught the youngest daughter of a Mrs Mary Moore up to some petty childhood misdemeanour. Swinow gave the child a severe telling-off and concluded with words along the lines of, 'and I'll make you sorry for what you have done.'

The next day, according to Mary Moore, the child was: 'suddainely stricken with a great deale of torment, called for a little beere, but ere they could come with it, the use of her tongue was gone, with all her limbs, pressing to vomit, and such torments, that no eyes could looke on her without compassion. Her mother comming home with a sad heart, beheld her childe, using what meanes could be, but no ease till eleaven or twelve a Clock at night she fell into a slumber and slept till six in the morning; as soon as Berwick gates were opened her mother sent for Phisitions, both of soule and body, with the Lady Selby, Colonell Fenwicks Widow, with other friends, who forthwith came to behold this sad sight, with many others that came to the childe waking out of herself, which was without present torment, but had lost the use of both limbs, tongue, stomacke, onely smiled on them, and signed, that we could understand she had all her other senses very perfect, but would let nothing come within her mouth of any nourishment, for her jawes were almost closed: Physitians gave their advice, with other friends; and what could be had, was gotten for her: but her signes from the beginning were, away with these Doctors Drugs, God had layd it on her, and God would take it off her.'

The child made a full recovery within a day or two but the terrifying train of events was not over: 'Her eldest Brother upon S. Johns day at night in the Christmas following betwixt the hours of 1 and 2 was taken exceedingly ill, that it was thought he would not live: the next morning he was a little eased of his extremity and pain, but both his stomack and the use of his legs taken from him, so that he was forced to have help to put on his cloathes, was lifted into a chaire where sat all day long, but could neither eate nor drinke any thing, but a little milke or water, or sowre milke. He consumed away to nothing, yet not heart-sicke; but would reason, talke and laugh with any friend as if nothing ailed him. His mother now being prest downe with sorrow, sent do the Doctors both at Newcastle, Durham, and Edenborough, not doubting or suspecting any unnaturall disease; the Physitians all agreed by the course of nature he could not live a month to an end, which was sad news to his sorrowful Mother, God knows.' The boy, also, recovered.

The fits continued at intervals into the spring, by which time the girl was experiencing visions of angels guarding her against attacks by giant boars and dragons. At this point Mrs Moore sent for a man named John Hulton, who was thought to be something of a wizard himself, and asked for his advice. Hulton listened to all the evidence, cast a few spells himself and announced that the trouble was being caused by Dorothy Swinow who held a grudge against the children.

Mrs Moore took her case to the magistrates of Newcastle, who threw them out as being utterly groundless. She then tried Berwick and the authorities there ordered the arrest of Swinow and had Hulton thrown into prison for good measure. However, Dorothy Swinow was the widow of a respected army officer, Colonel Swinow, and had friends in high places. She was released from Berwick prison within a few days, but Hulton died of fever in prison before his release.

In 1650 Mrs Moore tried the authorities at Durham. They took the case seriously enough to issue a warrant for Swinow's arrest, but the authorities in Northumberland refused to implement it and Dorothy Swinow went free.

That same year another woman was put on trial in Newcastle for witchcraft. This farmer's wife, Margaret White, confessed that she had served the Devil for five years. She said that she had enjoyed sex with Satan twice, apparently his sexual organ was enormous and ice-cold. White said that in return for her sexual favours the Devil had assured her that she would never suffer hunger. She claimed to be part of a group of witches who were active across Northumberland. Despite this confession, made without any apparent pressure and certainly no torture, the magistrates let White go since nobody had come forward with evidence that they had been harmed by her in any way.

The hunting of witches took a serious turn in that same year when a man came over the border from Scotland, bringing with him a reputation for being able to find and identify witches. When he arrived in Newcastle, the man convinced the city council that the place was rife with devil worship and witchcraft. They seem to have been persuaded when he produced a list of names. In all, 30 women and one man were arrested on the witchfinder's instructions and brought for trial.

When procedings opened, the 'trial' took a most unusual form. Instead of seeking out witnesses or evidence, the magistrate handed over to the witchfinder. He then conducted his own method of proving a person to be a witch or not. This consisted of having them stripped to the waist so that he could inspect their naked bodies at close quarters. He then produced a pin with which he stabbed the suspects. Those that bled were innocent, those who did not bleed were guilty.

Of those on trial, 15 were found to be guilty by this method and were sent to be hanged on the traditional execution ground of Town Moor, now the site of St James' Park football stadium. The witchfinder claimed his reward of 20/- in silver for each witch convicted. He was paid, but the gentry of the Northumberland countryside were rather disturbed by the fact that a man, and a Scot at that, could be paid such a handsome sum of money for the conviction of a witch when the only evidence against the suspect was his own test. When the witchfinder tried to ply his trade in the smaller towns of the county, he was sent packing back to Scotland.

More fortunate in that fatal year of 1650 was Elizabeth Simpson of Tynemouth. On 15 February she was hauled up in front of a magistrate, Luke Killingworth, accused of being a charmer, who predicted the future for payment, and of practising witchcraft. The main witness was Michael Mason of Tynemouth, who declared that: 'On 20th of January last, Elisabeth, wife of George Simpson of Tynemouth, fisher, came into his house and asked a pott full of small beare from Frances Mason, daughter to this informer; and, she refusing, the said Elisabeth threatened to make her repent. He saith that upon the next day the said Frances lost the use of one of her leggs, and, within foure dayes after, the use of the other; where-upon she, becoming lame, was necessitated to keep her bed, where she did lay miserably tormented, crying out that the said Elisabeth did pinch her heart and pull her in pieces; but, this informer getting blood from the said Elisabeth, she hath ever since continued quiett in her bed without any torture, but she doth not recover the use of her limmes, but pines away in a lamentable manner.'

Another typical case comes from 1661 when the unfortunate Jane Watson was tried in front of Sir John Marley, Mayor of Newcastle, on 10 October. The only witness was Winifrid Ogle of Winlington Whitehouse, who said: 'that aboute three of the clocke in the afternoone yesterday, she heareing that two of the children of Mr. Jonas Cudworth was at the house of Mr. Thomas Sherburn, watchmaker, in great paine, being bewitched, she came to see them and found them in great extrimity; and one of the said children and one Jane Pattison, who was then there cryed out they see the witch Jane Watson, and the child said the witch brought her an apple and was very ernest to have it, and presently after the people of the house cryed, "Fire, fire!" upon which this informant see something like a flash of fire on the farr side of the roome, and she see a round thing like fire goe towards the chimney, and the said childe was severall times speechles, and in great torment and paine, and that halfe of the apple the child spoak of was found att the bedfoote.'

The 1663 trial of Dorothy Stranger of Newcastle was recorded in more detail, perhaps because it ended with a hanging. The case was heard on 10 November in front of Sir James Clavering.

The first witness was Mrs Jane Milburne, who declared that: 'aboute a month agoe, shee sent her maid to one Daniell Strangers, of this towne, cooper, to get some caskes cooped; and when her servant came there, Dorothy, his wife, did say to her, "What was the reason that your dame did not invite her to the wedding supper?" And further said, that she would make her repent itt and deare to her. This informant sayth that Fryday gone a seaven night, about 8 o'clock att night, she being alone and in chamber, there appeared to her something in the perfect similitude and shape of a catt. And the said catt did leape at her face, and did vocally speake with a very audible voyce, and said that itt had gotten the life of one in this howse and came for this informer life, and would have itt before Saturday night. To which she replyed, "I defye the, the devil, and all his works." Upon which the catt did vanish. And upon Saturday last, aboute 8 of the clock in the morneing, she goeing downe to the seller for to draw a quart of beare, and, opening the seller dore, which was locked, she visibly did see the said Dorothy Stranger standing in the seller, leaneing with her armes upon one of the hodgheads, and said then to this informer, "Theafe, art thow there yett? Thy life I seeke, thy life I will have": and had a small rope in her hand, and did attemp to putt it over her heade aboute her neck, but she did hinder her with her hands. Further, she did take upp a quart pot and demanded a drinke, butt she would give her none. Whereupon the said Dorothy said that she would make her rue itt. To which this informer replyed that she defyed her and all her disciples. And Stranger answered againe, "Although thow be strong in faith, He overcome itt att the last." Upon Sunday last, aboute one of the clocke, this informer putting on her clothes in her chamber to goe to church, there did appear to her a catt of the same shape as the former, and did leap att her throat and said, "Theafe, I'll not overcome ye as yett." To which this informer replyed, "I hope in God un never shall." And the said catt did bite her arme and did hold itt very fast, and made a great impression in her arme with her teeth and did lett her hold goe and dis-appeared. And yesterday in the afternoone, aboute two of the clock, this informer comeing downe the stares, the said catt did violently leape aboute her neck and shoulders, and was soe ponderous that she was not able to support itt, but did bring her downe to the ground and kept her downe for the space of a quarter of an houre. And was soe infirme and disenabled that the power of both body and tongue were taken from her. And the last night, aboute 9 of the clocke, this informer being in bedd with her husband, the said Dorothy did in her perfect forme appear to her and tooke hold of the bed clothes and endevored to powle them of but could not. And then and there the said Stranger tooke hold of her arme and pulled her, and would have pulled her out of bed if her husband had not held her fast, and did nip and bite her armes very sore and tormented her body soe intollerably that she could nott rest all the night and was like to teare her very heart in peeces, and this morneing left her. And this informant veryly beleives that the said catt which appeared to her was Dorothy Stranger and non else. And she haveing a desire to see her did this morneing send for the said Dorothy, butt she was very loth to come, and comeing to her she gott blood of her at the said Stranger's desire, and since hath been pritye well.'

The same witness continued saying that a few days later: 'She being in bedd with her husband, aboute one of the clock in the morneing, the said Dorothy Stranger, in her own shape, appeared to this informer in the room where she was lyeing, the dores being all lock fast, and said to her, "Jane, Jane, art thou awaken?" She replyed, "Yes." Upon which the said Stranger answered, "I am come here to aske of the forgiveness for the wrong I have done the, and if thow will never troble me for whatt I have formerly done to thee, I doe promise never to molest or troble thee as long as thow lives." Upon the speakeing of which words she did vanish away. Aboute a month before she appeared as aforesaid, this informer being sitting alone in her howse, in a roome two storey high, there did then violently come rushing in att one of the paines of the window a grey catt And itt did transforme ittselfe into the shape of the said Dorothy Stranger, in the habitt and clothes she weares dayly, haveing an old black hatt upon her head, a greene waistcoate, and a brownish coloured petti- coate. And she said, "Thou gott blood of me, but I will have blood of thee before I goe." And she did flye violentlye upon this informer and did cut her over the joynts of the little finger of both her hands and did scratch her and gott blood. And haveing a black handercheife aboute her necke, she did take itt away, and never see the same since, and did then vanish away.'

Another witness was Elizabeth, Dorothy's sister-in-law. She gave evidence that: 'about six or seaven yeares agoe, her daughter Jane, then wife to Oswald Milburne, baker and brewer, being in the Sandhill, did meet with Dorothy Stranger, who said to her, "Thou shalt never see the Sandhill againe." And comeing home imediatly, she fell sick and lanwished above a yeare and dyed. And in her sicknes tooke very sad and lamentable fitts, and did cry out most hydeously, saying, "Ah, that witch-theafe, my ant Dorothy, is like to pull out my heart. Doe not yow see her? Doe not yow see her, my ant Dorothy, that witch?" And to her very last howre cry out of the said Dorothy Stranger.'

Despite the execution of Dorothy Stranger, Northumberland remained remarkably free of trials for witchcraft and there were even fewer convictions. Unlike East Anglia which saw dozens of executions, Northumberland had only a handful of witches sent to the gallows — burning at the stake was never in fashion in the North.

The evidence against Katherine Currey given in 1664 was not strong enough to persuade magistrate Sir James Clavering. It consisted mostly of a statement from William Thompson of Newcastle which read: 'that his daughter Alice, of the age of 17, hath beene for six weeks last by past most strangfully and wonderfully handled, insoemuch that she does continually cry out of one Katherine Currey, alias Potts, that wrongs her, saying, "Doe you not see her? Doe you not see her, where the witch theafe stands?" And she doth continually cry out that she pulls her heart; she pricks her heart, and is in the roome to carry her away. By reason whereof she is in great danger of her life. Ellinor Thompson sayth, that by the space of these seaven yeares bypast, she hath beene trobled by one Katherine Currey, widdow, severall tymes appearing in the night to her. And the weeke before Fasterne-evening gone a twelve month she came to this informer in the markett and layd her hands upon this informer's shoulder and sayd, "My peck of meall sett thy kill on fire." And within two dayes after the kill was on fire to her great losse and damage.'

Also in 1664 a Mrs Pepper was put on trial 'For using Charms, etc', a crime less serious than witchcraft. The evidence against her was given by Margaret Pyle, wife to a miner. Mrs Pyle declared: 'that aboute halfe a yeare agoe, her husband, being not well, sent his water to Mrs Pepper, a midwife, and one that uses to cast water. And the same day Mrs Pepper came to see him and did give him a little water in a bottle to tast, which he took and tasted, and forbad him to drink much of itt, but reserve itt to take when he tooke his fitts; and desired him to goe to the dore, which he did at her request. And imediately after Mrs Pepper and Tomisin Young did bring him with his leggs traileing upon the ground into the house. And he was in the fitt by the space of one houre and a halfe and was most strangely handled. And the said Mrs Pepper did take water and throwed it upon his face and touke this informer's child and another suck-ing child and laid them to his mouth. And shee demand-ing the reason why she did soe, she replyed that the breath of the children would suck the evill spirrit out of him, for he was possessed with an evill spirritt; and she said she would prove itt either before mayor or ministers that he was bewitched.'

Corroborating evidence came from Elizabeth, wife of Richard Rotherford, a tailor, who said: 'that she found Robert Pyle in a very sad condicion, lookeing with a distracted looke, every part of his body shaking and tremblinge, being deprived of the use of his body and senceces. Where there was then there one Mrs Pepper, a midwife, and she did see her call for a bottle of holy water and tooke the same and sprinkled it upon a redd hott spott which was upon the back of his right hand; and did take a silver crucifix out of her breast and lay itt upon the said spott. And did then say that shee knewe by the said spott what his disease was and did take the said crucifix and putt itt in his mouth.'

The most spectacular witchcraft trial in Northumberland took place in 1673. In that year what was alleged to be an entire coven was arrested and put on trial. The coven consisted of: Margaret Aynsley; Michael Aynsley; John Crauforth; Anne Driden; Anne Foster; Magaret Milburne; Elizabeth Pickering; Lucy Thompson; Anne Usher and William Wright. All 11 were accused by the notorious witch-hunter Anne Armstrong of Haltwhistle.

Anne Armstrong first accused Anne Baites of Morpeth not of being a witch herself, but of frequenting witches' meetings. Having got Baites into prison, Armstrong persuaded her to give evidence in which she named the members of the alleged coven. This evidence consisted of claims that at the meetings the witches danced with the Devil and turned themselves into the shape of a cat, a hare, a greyhound and a bee. They took delight in 'letting the divell see how many shapes they could turn into.' The witches reached the meetings, apparently, by riding on wooden dishes and in egg shells. The meetings were held at a great dining table with 'theire protector which thev call'd their god, sitting, at the head of the table in a gold chaire, as she thought; and a rope hanging over the roome which every one touch'd three several times and what ever was desired was sett upon the table, of several kindes of meate and drinke, and when they had eaten, she that was last drew the table and kept the reversions.'

The case was dismissed when no evidence could be found that the coven had done harm to anyone.

In 1683 another witch was brought to trial. Margaret Stothard, the witch of Edlingham, was hauled up in front of Henry Ogle JP on charges of carrying out wicked

The parish church of Edlingham, the scene of a classic witch trial in 1683.

deeds by means of witchcraft. Ogle demanded that witnesses be brought forward who were able to give firm evidence of actual instances of witchcraft.

The first witness to come forward was John Mills. He said that one night as he lay in his bed a terrific blow hit his house, as if a great gust of wind had come from nowhere. At the same moment something fell onto his bed uttering a piercing shriek like a frightened cat. Mills said that he had sat up, whereupon an eerie green light had begun to glow at the foot of the bed. Out of this glow had emerged the figure of Margaret Stothard, gesturing and pointing at him. Mills had to admit that apart from a broken night's sleep he had suffered no ill effects.

Next up was William Collingwood, a farmer. He said that the wife of one of his farmhands, a Jane Carr, had a sickly baby. The baby had been taken to the witch of Edlingham, who had lifted the baby up and put her mouth to that of the child, all the while making strange clucking and chirping noises. Had the child died? No, it had actually got better and was still alive.

The third witness was Jacob Mills, a servant at Edlingham Castle. He said that a friend's child, Alexander Nicholl of Lorbottle, had died after Margaret Stothard visited the Nicholl household and waved a white handkerchief when leaving – obviously a curse. Could Nicholl come forward to give first-hand evidence? Apparently not.

Fourth to appear was Isabel Maine of Shawdon who stated that the previous spring her cow's milk had gone sour. She had called in Margaret Stothard to help with the problem. Stothard had gone off into the woods and returned with a bag of leaves and herbs. She had told Maine to mix the leaves in with some hay and feed it to the cow each morning for a week. The cow's milk promptly returned to its healthy condition.

Mr Ogle then called proceedings to an end. He pronounced himself unable to decide if Margaret Stothard really was a witch or not. Even if she were, she was not doing any harm to anybody. The case was dismissed.

It was a wizard, not a witch, who made his mark at Morpeth. Michael Scott of Balwearie in Fife was counted to be the greatest wizard in the world, having travelled widely and learned all there was to learn. One day he rode over the hills on his magical black stallion to pay a visit to Morpeth. The town council met to decide what spell they should ask him to perform for them in payment for providing him with free food and lodging during his stay.

After much debate, it was finally decided that they should ask him to bring the tide to Morpeth. At this time the small wooden trading ships were not able to get up the River Wansbeck to Morpeth itself, but instead had to unload their cargoes down at the river's mouth where they would be put onto carts and laboriously hauled along the road to Morpeth. The town council were very jealous of Newcastle, for the merchant ships could sail right up the Tyne to the docks of Newcastle. If only the ships could reach Morpeth, the council believed, their little town would be as prosperous as Newcastle.

Michael Scott listened to the request gravely and nodded his agreement. He asked the council to send the fastest runner in all of Morpeth to him.

'Now then young man,' said Scott when the runner arrived. 'You must go down to the seashore at Wansbeck where the river meets the sea. When the tide is at its highest you must start running up the path that runs alongside the river. The tide will follow you till you get to Morpeth. But there is one thing you must do without fail. On no account must you look back. Once you do so the tide will follow you no further.'

The next morning the runner went down to Wansbeck, 10 miles downstream from Morpeth, and waited. When an old local fishermen assured him that the tide was at its highest the man set off at a steady jog toward Morpeth. He had not gone far when he felt water splashing at his heels. Then he heard the sounds of waves breaking, as if a great storm was blowing. The surf was only inches behind him, throwing spray forward over his head and threatening to engulf him. Next came the shrieks and cries of the water spirits who did not want the tide to flow inland to Morpeth. The runner had got as far as Bothal before the tumult behind him became so terrifying and sounded so close that he inadvertently threw a glance over his shoulder. At once the tumult died down, the waves ceased crashing and the spirits screaming. And the tide stopped advancing. That is why the tide reaches only so far as Bothal, never coming inland to Morpeth.

The first image of a witch that can be discarded, therefore, is the typical witch depicted in children's books. Witches never wore tall, conical, black hats nor dressed in black cloaks. Their outfits might have been old-fashioned, but that was generally due to their old age more than anything else. Some witches did dress for effect, preferring outlandish outfits to help create an image of strangeness which would impress upon their neighbours the feeling that they were a little odd. Some had a special item of clothing that they claimed was linked to their work. One, sadly not from Northumberland, who was active in the 1840s and 1850s, always wore an old blue overcoat when 'doing magic'. This magic was not, as we have seen, of the type that would turn men into frogs or cause people to vanish.

Nor is the witch of the horror movies any closer to reality. This view of witches as the spawn of Satan is based very much upon studies conducted by religious men in the 16th and 17th centuries, mostly in continental Europe. It was from these sources that the classic image of a witch flying through the air on a broomstick is drawn. This interpretation of witches saw them flying off to attend ceremonies at which they worshipped the Devil in diabolical ceremonies of depravity and – sometimes – violence. In Europe the belief in the demonic origins of witchcraft led to the executions of thousands of women and men accused of consorting with the Devil. In Britain there were executions and

The River Wansbeck downstream of Morpeth. The river is tidal for only a short distance because a wizard's magic failed to work properly.

imprisonment of witches, but the authorities took a rather more pragmatic view of the subject. Being a witch was not in itself a crime, though committing a crime through witchcraft was counted to be more heinous than if the crime had been committed by normal means.

Nor, in all likelihood, is the modern religion of Wicca very closely linked to witches. Wicca claims to be descended from the beliefs of old-time witches and portrays them as a surviving pagan cult which has managed to continue in the otherwise solidly Christian lands of Britain. It is an attractive theory, but it depends for its credibility upon the writings of a single man: Gerald Gardner. After his retirement from government service, Gardner moved to the New Forest where he claimed to have come into contact with an ancient coven of witches. Gardner was, he says, initiated into the cult and allowed to see and copy out the *Book of Shadows*, on which he based his subsequent career as the founder of modern Wicca.

Gardner's version of witchcraft involved esoteric rituals, including sinister robes, nudity, sexual intercourse, ritual bondage and chants of obscure meaning. All these subjects had been a great interest of Gardner's before he had met the New Forest witches and had been one reason why he had been treated with some coolness during his career. More than one reasearcher suspects that Wicca was more a product of Gardner's imagination than of any ancient pagan cult.

So if these ideas are flawed, what is the real explanation for the many theories and apparently firm beliefs in witches and witchcraft that lie behind the Northumberland stories. The truth is both more prosaic and more interesting than the various explanations that have gained popularity over the years.

The case of Margaret Stothard, the witch of Edlingham, is in many ways typical of the real accounts of witches that have surfaced over the years. She came from, and mixed with, the ordinary farming folk of rural England. The services that she provided to her neighbours were concerned with the health of children and of livestock. Typically, a witch would be called upon to deal with a wide range of health and welfare issues. She would also be asked to locate lost or stolen items and sometimes to identify the thief as well. Usually witches did not ask for payment for their services. Instead, they expected a share of meat at the next pig-killing or to be given some apples at harvest time. In other words they took no money, but were paid in kind in the sorts of goods that humble rural folk would have to spare from time to time.

It is beyond doubt that in centuries gone by there lived dozens of witches in Northumberland who were believed to have all sorts of magical powers. Some of these powers can be explained in fairly rational terms. When the witch of Edlingham cured a cow with herbs she was almost certainly using a knowledge of natural medicinal chemicals to be found in certain plants. Other aspects of witchy power were almost certainly achieved through hypnotism. For instance, a man who had swindled another at a fair in Yorkshire was caused to dance without stopping by a passing witch until he returned the disputed money.

Witches could also rely on the sheer power of their reputations to achieve results. The news that a powerful witch had been called in to locate stolen property was often enough to cause the thief to return the stolen goods. Nobody wanted to be on the receiving end of a finding spell.

Witches, and the wizards or cunning men who were their male counterparts, were not always as benign as this image might suggest. Some would extract gifts from their neighbours by threatening to cast a spell over their livestock. The powers and gifts of a witch could be put to use causing mischief and disease just as certainly as they could be put to use for good. If one set of herbs could cure a cow, another set could make it sick or even kill it. Some witches relied more on the negative aspects of their powers than on the beneficial effects and became greatly feared as a result. It was these witches that were denounced to the authorities by their neighbours and who ended up in trouble. The Witch of Seaton Delaval presumably fell into this category.

Other tales told about witches may belong more in the realms of folklore than genuine mystery. The great Michael Scott, for instance, was a real person, though his visit to Morpeth is not recorded in any historical document. Scott was born in about 1180 and by 1210 was teaching at the University of Paris. In 1217 he moved to Toledo in Spain where he studied Arabic manuscripts taken from the Moslem dynasties that then ruled southern Spain. He later moved to Sicily where he studied astrology and delved further into Arab knowledge. He seems to have returned to Scotland around 1245, though this is disputed. It was probably his great knowledge of Arab learning that gained him a reputation for magical ability.

As for Meg of Meldon, there is very little in her story that ties her to any actual feats of witchcraft. It seems that her supposed magical abilities were more related to a knack for making money out of the misfortunes of others and a ruthless streak that enabled her to take advantages that others might prefer to pass up. Perhaps she was called a witch and accused of being in league with the Devil by friends of her victims.

That said, there are other aspects of witch power that are well attested in the records, but which simply cannot be explained by a knowledge of medicinal herbs, hypnosis or the like. To a modern researcher these accounts read more like demonstrations of ESP, clairvoyance or even psychokinetics. However, these alleged powers are not recognised by modern science and remain as mysterious as witches ever were.

CHAPTER 7

MYSTERIOUS BEASTS

Northumberland is a county of mysterious beasts. Some of these are solid and real enough, one could see them almost any day that they choose. Others belong to the realms of the truly mysterious, living in the world of dreams past and ages yet to come.

That the great white cattle of Chillingham exist there can be no doubt. However, where they originated, how they got to Chillingham and what types of magical powers they may have are altogether far more mysterious.

According to some versions of the story, the unique white cattle of Chillingham are descended from a herd of wild cattle that were included in the 330-acre hunting park of Chillingham when it was first enclosed as a private hunting ground of the adjacent castle in 1344. Unfortunately for this theory, the true wild cows, or aurochs, went extinct in Britain around 1000 BC, so the chances of a small herd surviving the intervening 2,000 years to the foundation of the park are remote.

Chillingham Park contains the ruins of several Roman buildings, none of which have yet been properly excavated by archaeologists, and has led some to suggest that the white cattle are of Roman origin. Cattle were certainly raised in Northumberland in the Roman period. Indeed, the Roman army during the second century, and probably at other times,

A group of the famous white cattle of Chillingham, the origins of which are shrouded in mystery.

The wild white cattle of Chillingham live in the great park of Chillingham without almost any contact with humans, other than for the distribution of winter feed in particularly cold weather.

specified stewed beef as a fairly major element in the diet of the soldier. The presence of thousands of soldiers on Hadrian's Wall and in the forts behind it would have provided a ready market for local men raising cattle in what is now Northumberland. There is some evidence that the number of cattle in northern Britain increased significantly after Hadrian's Wall had been built.

Others believe that the herd is descended from mediaeval cattle which were living wild in the area. The oldest known reference to the white cattle comes in a manuscript thought to have been produced in about the year AD 700. It shows a bull with the unmistakable cream-coloured coat and red ears of the Chillingham breed, and would seem to indicate that the herd is derived from a local breed that once flourished in Northumberland farms but has since been replaced by more productive and docile breeds as farm stock. Whatever their origins, the white cattle have grazed near Chillingham and have been owned by the earls of Tankerville for their entire recorded history.

The earliest detailed records of the herd were kept in the 1780s. At that time some calves were born with black ears, but these were removed for slaughter by the keeper and not allowed to breed. By the 1850s the modern coat pattern with red ears and some shoulder spotting was well established. The cattle live wild, and, other than removing juveniles deemed to be inferior, there is no control over breeding.

Foot-and-mouth disease has almost wiped out the white cattle of Chillingham on two occasions, but fortunately enough young calves are born to boost the population and ensure the breed's survival into the 21st century.

There is usually a 'king bull' who dominates all the other animals and who alone mates with the cows. Some years the herd has divided into two or three groups, each led by a bull who mates with the females in the section of the herd that he rules. Fights between the bulls are usually more by way of threat and bluff than actual physical fighting. The rivals will come to within a few yards of each other before pawing the ground and bellowing. This may go on for some minutes before one or other backs away. More serious fights take place when neither bull backs off. Then the rivals will charge at each other to lock horns and wrestle head to head for some minutes. Usually there are breaks of up to 10 minutes between bouts of these locked horn contests, which can continue for hours on end.

During the 20th century only three bulls were killed in these fights for dominance. In 1939 one bull was found lying dead, having suffered horrific injuries to its chest and flank. The internal organs had been reduced to pulp in such a way that the butting and pounding by the victor must have continued some time after the unfortunate bull had died. Such a level of violence is exceptional. The wild cattle are, however, dangerous beasts. A mother will attack without warning if a human gets too close to a calf. This can happen very easily as young calves lie down motionless in the long grass of the park and cannot be seen until the walker is close to them.

Disaster has threatened the herd on at least three occasions within living memory. In 1947 the worst winter in a generation saw snowdrifts of up to 40 feet deep form across the park and there was almost no hay left anywhere in Northumberland. When the snow melted there were only five bulls and eight cows left alive: no calves survived. That savage winter had a long-term effect for no cow became pregnant for more than a year. The numbers then began to increase rapidly until by 1981 there were 59 cattle. In 1967 an outbreak of foot-and-mouth disease came to within two miles of the park. The park was sealed off and armed guards patrolled the area to ensure that no hoofed animals nor humans entered. In 2001 another outbreak of the same disease got to within six miles, but again it did not enter the park.

After the 1967 foot-and-mouth outbreak a bull and two cows were moved to a location in Scotland to form a second herd. This reserve herd is thriving, providing a vital back-up herd in case any disaster should strike Chillingham. Another move to safeguard the future of the herd was taken in 1971 when the ninth earl of Tankerville established the Chillingham Wild Cattle Association to care for the cattle. With financial aid from the Duke of Northumberland, the association has subsequently purchased woodland around the park. The association now opens the park to the public on most days of the year, as detailed on the website, www.chillinghamwildcattle.org.uk.

High up on the southern side of the Simonside Hills is a cave known as Croppie's Hole. It is some miles from the nearest road and is rarely visited, but in years gone by it was notorious as home to an old male fox of legendary cunning. The fox had almost been caught by a young animal from the hunters' hounds and had lost half his tail to their jaws. The cropped tail was responsible for his name of 'Croppie'. For years Croppie eluded the hunters and hounds, always managing to slip away no matter how close the pursuers got. Then, in the 1860s, Croppie was put up by hounds on the lower slopes of Simonside. For once the wily fox did not head up into his native hills, but bolted east down Coquetdale. Sensing that at last they might have him, the hunters gave chase. The ride proved to be a long and arduous one. One by one the huntsmen fell out of the chase, either through fatigue or through a tumble at a fence or hedge. Still Croppie ran on, until he emerged out on the wide beach of Amble Sands. By this time there was only one hunter still giving chase. Glancing back at his tormentor, Croppie raced on to plunge into the surf with a strange, shrieking cry. The hunter pulled up on the beach and scanned the waters for some sign of the fox. However, Croppie was never seen again.

The tale of the Laidley Worm of Bamburgh is a mystery in more ways than one. The story was first published by the vicar of Norham, Revd Robert Lambert, in 1778. Lambert said that he had found various versions of the story being told, usually in verse form, across Northumberland. He speculated that the verses might derive from a lost original by the great mountain bard, Duncan Frasier. Frasier is known to have been active around the year 1270, but, although he was famous in his own day and for generations afterward, no examples of his work are known to have survived.

The story of the Laidley Worm begins at Bamburgh Castle with a classic conflict between a virtuous daughter and a wicked stepmother, but this tale has a curious twist.

Unfortunately, Lambert is known to have been guilty of tidying up many of the stories he recorded. In some cases this involved merely explaining some of the more obscure dialect words for his readers. In other instances Lambert changed elements of the story, especially endings, to make them more satisfying or to tie up loose ends left in his originals. In a few instances he seems to have invented the entire story that he claimed to have heard from the lips of a local storyteller.

The story, as told by Lambert, begins when Childy Wynde, the son and heir to the king of Northumbria, travels far away on a diplomatic mission. Wynde leaves behind him his father, a king well into his middle age, and his sister, Margaret. Margaret is a beautiful and virtuous young damsel who cares for her father and acts as Lady of Bamburgh. However, the king soon meets a young woman with whom he falls deeply in love. He marries her and brings her back to Bamburgh as his queen.

The pretty new queen was, as is the way in these tales, a wicked sorceress of great power. The virtuous Margaret alone can see her for what she really is, so the new queen decides to get rid of Margaret. A day or two later Margaret vanishes and a torn fragment of her cloak is found caught on a crag near a dangerous part of the cliffs on the seaward side of the castle. Everyone assumes that she slipped and fell to her death.

A few days later a terrible serpent takes up residence on the Spindlestone Heugh, a rocky outcrop a few miles west of Bamburgh. The monstrous serpent demanded and was given the milk of seven cattle to drink each day. The milk was poured into a stone trough at the foot of the Spindlestone Heugh. Despite this tribute being paid regularly, the worm's poisonous breath blighted the land for seven miles around the heugh so that nothing would grow there.

Hearing of the terrible plague affecting his ancestral lands, Childy Wynde hurried home to slay the monster. He raced out to do battle, but as he drew his sword Childy Wynde was amazed to hear the monster speak. The worm asked the young man to kiss it three times. Childy Wynde carried out the request and the monster transformed into his sister, Margaret. The pair then hurried to Bamburgh to confront the wicked queen. When Childy Wynde accused the queen, she screamed and transformed into a toad which spat out poison. A well-placed kick threw the toad out of the castle, but thereafter it lurked around the great rock on which the castle stood, spitting its venom at unwary passers-by.

Opinion is divided as to how much of this tale was an original folk tale and how much was invented by Lambert. Until quarrying in the 19th century tore most of it away, the Spindlestone Heugh had ridges around it that did look as if they had been moulded by a gigantic snake coiling around it. In addition it had a huge hollow stone at its base that could easily have held the milk from seven cows. There was also a local story about an old witch who took the form of a poisonous toad and lurked around Bamburgh looking for victims at whom to spit venom.

Some believe that Lambert took these genuine elements and added them to the old Welsh story of Kemp Owyne. In this tale a wicked stepmother transforms her virtuous stepdaughter into a dragon, who can be restored to human form only by three kisses from a knight. The knight in question is Kemp Owyne, who after various adventures and exploits does finally kiss the dragon, restoring her to her true form as a beautiful girl whom he promptly falls in love with.

On the other hand, the two stories are not quite identical – Margaret is said to be Childy Wynde's sister, not his beloved, for instance. Also the name of Childy Wynde seems to be taken from the old English word for young man plus a corrupted version of the name Owyne. Perhaps the tale really is a genuine Northumberland folk tale as Lambert claimed; it is a mystery that looks set never to be solved.

Another dragon is supposed to have lived in a wood just outside Longwitton. This monster arrived to take possession of three magic springs that lay in the wood. This was a huge inconvenience for the local people, who had made a tidy living from the many pilgrims who came to drink of the sacred waters. The local men set out to attack the dragon, but it beat them off with ease. It soon transpired that the dragon did no real harm to the surrounding countryside and was content to simply sit in the woodland and drink the waters of the three springs.

The woods outside Longwitton, where three sacred springs attracted the attentions of a ferocious dragon — but there may be more truth in this curious story than at first appears to be the case.

Some months later a knight came riding by and offered to kill the dragon for the villagers. The very next day he rode out to fight the dragon. The beast proved to be enormously strong, but ungainly and sluggish. The knight on his nimble warhorse was able to dart around to deliver wound after wound on the monster with ease. However, no matter how well he fought or how badly he wounded the dragon, the knight could not see any sign that his opponent was weakening. Perplexed, he drew off to think.

The next day the knight returned to the attack. He was now convinced that the dragon was possessed of some magic that explained its invulnerability. As he fought, the knight watched the dragon carefully. He soon spotted that whenever it was wounded the dragon would place its tail into the water flowing from the three sacred springs. Guessing that this was the source of the dragon's self-healing ability, the knight decided to try a trick.

On the third day that he went out to fight, the knight pretended to be wounded and fatigued by the previous two days of combat. Feigning an injured leg and weary arms, the knight fought badly and did not push home any attacks. Instead he crept slowly backward, luring the dragon further and further from the sacred springs. When he thought the dragon had come far enough, the knight leapt onto his horse and galloped quickly to get to the springs first. The dragon saw it had been tricked and attacked with great fury. It was no match for the knight, however, and soon it lay dead. The three sacred springs were restored to use and the grateful villagers hailed the knight as a hero.

This tale seems to be derived from the early days of Christianity in Northumberland. Early missionaries very often used the dragon as a symbol of pagan deities and their power. The book of Revelation features a battle between the Archangel Michael and the Devil in which the latter is described as a gigantic serpent. The sacred springs that feature so strongly in the tale seem to confirm this theory. Many of the pagan goddesses who preceded Christianity in this area were linked to sacred springs or wells, several of which had miraculous powers.

The tale of the Longwitton dragon should, therefore, be read as an allegory of the coming of Christianity to the village. A Christian outsider – the knight – destroys the pagan deity – the dragon – which has possession of the springs and so converts them to Christian use. The story as it stands is probably pure storytelling, but it may refer to a real conflict between pagan adherents and Christian converts sometime in the sixth or seventh centuries.

Other legendary animals of Northumberland are less easy to explain. At Preston there is said to be a guard dog that stalks the lanes of the village and the surrounding fields. The dog is said to be protective of natives of the village, but bitterly hostile to outsiders. It is said to have once been a real, living guard dog, as large as a donkey and as ferocious as a war dog, that was bred and brought up here. However, as it grew larger its owner

The lanes around the village of Preston are said to be patrolled by a guard dog that is friendly toward the locals, but hostile to outsiders.

The bridge at Rothbury, where a most peculiar cat has been seen.

grew frightened of the dog's awesome power and savage temper and he decided to get rid of it by feeding it poisoned meat. When the fatal meal was put in front of the dog, however, it howled in anger. The hound then snapped its chain, tore the owner limb from limb and ran off into the countryside. Ever since then the Preston hound has patrolled its territory and protected the human inhabitants.

Even more enigmatic is the cat of Rothbury. This creature is said to lurk around the bridge on the edge of the small town. No story is attached to it and no explanation given as to why this odd animal should slink about here, but it has been reported many times over the centuries.

CHAPTER 8

MYSTERIOUS SAINTS

That Northumberland is a land of saints cannot be disputed. However, mystery surrounds many aspects of Northumberland's conversion to Christianity, including the lives of the missionaries who achieved the feat and the way in which the conversion was carried out. The disputes and mysteries of the time now and then threatened to lead to wars. The controversies were deeply mired in politics and they have left their mark on the modern landscape in often surprising ways.

The basis for the earliest mysteries lies in the fact that nobody is entirely certain how Christian the area was after the first wave of missionary activity between about AD 250 and AD 400. We know that across most of Roman Britain there was a complex system of bishops with authority over local priests. Most bishops were based in walled cities and had duties relating to the secular government of the land. It is thought that by about AD 400 the vast majority of people in towns, and a large minority of people in the countryside, were Christian.

How effectively the new religion had penetrated the border lands around Hadrian's Wall is unclear. It is generally thought that most of the army was Christian, but beyond that nothing firm is known. After Britain became independent of the Roman Empire in AD 410 there followed several generations during which the Romano-British system of government continued to function reasonably well. As late as AD 550 there were bishops in several southern towns who continued to exercise spiritual leadership over their flocks.

In the north there was a burst of missionary activity that saw Christians pushing north into the barbarian lands to convert the pagan to Christianity. Very few written records of this process have survived and what there are was written down centuries later. The Irish seem to have been converted first and in AD 563 a team of Irish monks arrived on the island of Iona off the west coast of Scotland to begin the conversion of the northern lands.

Even as this process of converting the barbarians was underway, Christianity in Britain received a body blow with the migration of large numbers of pagan Germanic settlers to the south and east. These incomers became the English. Sometime in the sixth century they overthrew the existing political structure of post-Roman Britain and founded a number of pagan English kingdoms. What is now Northumberland then formed the heartland of the kingdom of Bernicia and centred on the royal stronghold of Bamburgh. When Bernicia was joined to Deira of southern Yorkshire, the new and much more powerful kingdom of Northumbria was created. For the next century Northumbria would be the leading English kingdom.

Although the ruins on Lindisfarne belong to a later date, they stand on the site of the monastery founded by St Aidan in 634.

How well Christianity had coped with these upheavals is unknown. Certainly it went into a serious decline in the north. The formal structure of bishops presiding over priests was utterly destroyed. Many Christians converted to the paganism of the incoming English, perhaps for political reasons. By the year 600 Northumbria was essentially a pagan land, though there were undoubtedly some Christians who had held on to their faith. There may even have been a few scattered and impoverished monasteries.

In 634 Oswald, a younger son of King Athelfrith, came to the throne. The young Oswald had been educated at Iona and had become a Christian. Once securely in power, Oswald sent a message back to Iona asking the monks there to send a team to convert Northumbria back to Christianity. The missionary team arrived and was led by St Aidan. Aidan's first move was to found a monastery on the island of Lindisfarne to act as a school and missionary powerhouse for the effort of conversion. He was made Bishop of Lindisfarne by Oswald.

The conversion had only just begun in earnest when King Oswald was killed in battle by the pagan King Penda of Mercia. Aidan received the news when he was walking past the east end of the wooden church that he had built just outside the king's fortress at Bamburgh – probably on the site of the modern parish church. He slumped back to lean on the wooden wall and died, apparently of shock. When the pagan Mercians rampaged across Northumberland they set fire to the church. The only part of it that remained unburned was the upright post against which Aidan had been leaning when he died.

Meanwhile, up in the hills far to the west, a shepherd lay down to sleep. Some time after midnight the shepherd suddenly awoke to find himself confronted by a vision of Aidan, whom he had once seen. The soul of Aidan was surrounded by angels who carried him upward to disappear from sight among the stars, as if carried up to heaven to sit with God. The name of that shepherd was Cuthbert. He took the vision to be a sign that he had been singled out by Aidan to continue his work of converting the pagans in Northumbria.

Having trained as a monk in the monastery of Melrose, then part of Northumberland, Cuthbert set out on his task. He converted thousands by the power of his oratory, and by 664 had become Prior of Lindisfarne. In that year a theological debate erupted into a violent dispute that forced Cuthbert into a crisis of faith. The court of King Oswiu was visited by a delegation from the Pope in Rome demanding that he accept the teachings and authority of the Pope.

The problem was that the Christian tradition that had survived the fall of Roman Britain and that had largely converted Northumbria by this date did not recognise the Pope to be anything other than the Bishop of Rome. He was not held to have authority of any kind over Christians outside Rome, who instead should be free to elect their own bishops, found their own monasteries and generally run their own spiritual affairs. The two sides disagreed most violently over the date on which Easter should be celebrated and the way that monks shaved their heads into a tonsure.

In 664 King Oswiu summoned all the clergy and noblemen of his kingdom to a great meeting at Whitby to discuss the problem. Cuthbert attended the crucial meeting. After long debate, some of it heated and at times almost violent, King Oswiu declared that he was siding with Rome. He said that the Pope had authority in spiritual matters, though he carefully retained the right to appoint the bishops and senior clergy of Northumbria for himself.

Cuthbert accepted the ruling and returned to Lindisfarne from where he continued to roam the kingdom, converting pagans and providing spiritual support to Christians. By the later 670s, however, he was thirsting for solitude in which to study and to worship God. He moved first to Thrush Island, but this was connected to Lindisfarne at low tide and did not provide him with the solitude he sought. Cuthbert therefore built himself a small chapel and hut on the more remote island of Inner Farne. He dug a well and constructed a sluice; he planted barley and vegetables to provide himself with food, miraculously keeping the birds away from his crops by talking to them. Cuthbert then built a small hut in which sailors could shelter if they came to Farne

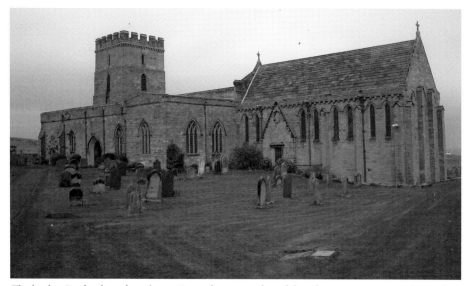

The church at Bamburgh stands on the site of a wooden structure burned down by rampaging pagans in the seventh century. One wooden pillar was miraculously saved from the conflagration.

to escape from a storm. Cuthbert's reputation for piety continued to draw pilgrims to Inner Farne and he welcomed them all to his humble hut and discussed God's word with them.

Numerous stories are told about Cuthbert's missionary travels around Northumbria. He was once approached by the nobleman Ilderton of Hilderton, whose wife was desperately ill at home. Cuthbert listened to the man and then said that by the time he got home his wife would have recovered. The man did not believe Cuthbert and begged him to come in person to administer a blessing. Cuthbert went as asked, but as he had said the woman was recovered by the time they arrived. Cuthbert cured another woman, named Hemma, at what is now Homilton. At Easington he consecrated a church that had been built by Elfled, a pious lady of some wealth.

On 20 May 685 Cuthbert was stood on Hadrian's Wall within his then diocese of Hexham when he had a vision. He saw King Egfrith of Northumbria being cut down and killed in battle by the Picts. Cuthbert hurried to find Queen Irminburg, who was then at Carlisle, to tell her of his vision. The queen ordered the noblemen to summon the troops left at home and so put Northumbria in a state of readiness for the Pictish attack that would to come if Egfrith was, indeed, dead. A messenger was sent riding hard to find Aldrith, the heir to the throne, to summon him home from a visit to the south.

News came a few days later that the king and most of his army had been ambushed and killed on the shores of Nechtansmere. The victorious King Breide of the Picts

In 686 the isolated Church Hill at Alnmouth was the site of the synod of Twyford, which was called to decide the future of St Cuthbert, the greatest missionary in Northumbria.

came rampaging south, calling on the Scots and Britons to join him, but Aldfrith and the Northumbrians were ready and the assault was driven off.

In 685 Cuthbert was elected Bishop of Hexham, replacing Bishop Tumbert who was ousted by the king for unspecified misdemeanours. Cuthbert reluctantly left Farne, but, having sorted out the confusion and mess left by his predecessor, wished to return to Farne in time for Christmas 686. Many of the clergy and laity of Northumberland had no wish for him to return to the life of a hermit, having far too much work for him to do. A great synod was held at Alnmouth to debate the issue. The synod was held in the minster of 'Twyford'. There is some mystery over the location of this minster. Today there is neither a ford across the river nor the remains of an ancient minster to be found anywhere near Alnmouth. The most likely explanation is that the minster stood on what is now Church Hill and that a ford over the Aln lay nearby. There was certainly an ancient Norman-style church on the hill, but this fell into disrepair around 1550 and by 1740 was a ruin. In 1806 a mighty storm lashed the coast. The waves smashed through the sandbanks off the mouth of the Aln, causing the river to change its course. A large section of Church Hill was brought down, taking with it the ruins of the Norman church and any archaeological remains that may have pinpointed it as the site of the minster of Twyford.

The synod agreed that Cuthbert could return to Farne, but only if he agreed to serve as Bishop of Lindisfarne and made himself available to give advice and arbitrate in disputes regarding the church in Northumbria. Reluctantly, Cuthbert agreed.

The 900-year-old doorway that marks the entrance to the monastery of Lindisfarne. St Cuthbert was made Bishop of Lindisfarne as an old man and spent the remainder of his life either on Lindisfarne or on the more remote island of Inner Farne.

179

The entrance to Cuddie's Cave in the remote Kyloe Hills. It is thought that the monks protecting St Cuthbert's body hid out here for some weeks when on the run from Viking marauders.

Finally, Cuthbert went back to Inner Farne. He was, by this date, an elderly man, being at least 60 years old. He died on Farne on 20 March the following year and was buried on Lindisfarne. By the time he died Cuthbert had achieved his mission and had made Northumbria a mostly Christian kingdom.

St Cuthbert's career as a wandering teacher of Christianity did not end with his death. In 875 a vast fleet of Vikings arrived in the Tyne to begin the systematic pillaging of Northumbria. Lindisfarne had already been raided once, in 793, and the monks knew that they had no chance of resisting a new attack. Desperate to save their relics, books and lives, the monks packed up everything – including the sacred body of St Cuthbert – and set off on foot. Seven young monks were given the especial task of carrying St Cuthbert's coffin and keeping it safe from the Vikings.

For seven long years the seven monks carried St Cuthbert's body around the north of England, always trying to keep out of the way of the rampaging Vikings, who were hunting them down to seize and destroy the sacred relics, thereby demoralising the Christians. Where they went and what they did is something of a mystery. There are a few glimpses of the monks recorded in manuscripts.

For some time they stayed in the cavern on the Kyloe Hills, which is now known as Cuddie's Cave – Cuddie being a familiar form of the name Cuthbert. The loyal villagers from round about brought food to the cave and came to pray at the coffin of St Cuthbert. The cave is still an atmospheric place, ringed as it is by stately pines and offering a fine view out across the lowlands to the west. It is easy to imagine the monks sitting here, warily watching the landscape for the campfires of roving Viking bands, flinching at the sound of approaching footsteps and praying desperately for salvation.

For a while, the coffin was hidden at Bellingham. When the coffin was taken up to be moved a spring of pure water welled up from the ground where it had rested. The water proved to be highly effective at helping wounds to heal. When I visited Bellingham in the winter of 2008, I met a lady who was taking her child to the spring to wash a grazed knee. 'That will make sure it mends soon enough,' the woman said.

At Tillmouth the coffin was laid in a small wooden chapel. The chapel that stands today, where the Till enters the Tweed, dates to about 500 years after the coffin rested here and is dedicated to St Cuthbert. There was on this spot, until 1773, what was described as 'Cuthbert's Stone Boat', though it was probably a stone sarcophagus. It measured nine feet three inches by three feet three inches and was held to be the stone boat in which Cuthbert had miraculously floated down the Tweed from Melrose as a young man. In 1773 a local farmer decided to haul the stone boat to his farm to serve as a receptacle for storing pickled beef. As the farmer arrived with his horses and harness to drag the stone boat away, the saint appeared in the sky and sent down a thunderbolt to destroy the boat, preferring to shatter it into fragments than see it profaned.

Cuthbert's remote sanctuary on Inner Farne fared rather better than his stone boat. After Cuthbert's death, the island, its hut and chapel were taken over by Aethelwald, a monk from Ripon who craved solitude. Aethelwald was credited with the power to calm the stormy seas around the Farne Islands by the power of prayer alone. He died in 699 and was followed by a monk named Felgild, who suffered a serious skin disease until he took up residence on Inner Farne, where it was miraculously cured. Felgild was followed by Billfrith in around 730.

What happened next is unclear, as the records of Lindisfarne were lost in the Viking raids. Other manuscripts and sources make occasional reference to a hermit living on Inner Farne through the eighth and ninth centuries, but the next firm date is 1083 when a hermit named Edulf came to Inner Farne. He found the place deserted and the buildings in ruins. With the aid of monks from Lindisfarne, Edulf repaired the chapel and built a new hut. By 1135 Edulf had died and had been replaced by Aelric of Durham. This Aelric was clearly a different sort of hermit as he kept servants to look after him.

The next occupant was also somewhat unusual in that he brought a friend to live with him. Aelwin and Bartholomew lived on Inner Farne until they had a serious argument in 1151 and Aelwin stormed off to Lindisfarne, leaving Bartholomew to a further 42 years of solitude on the island.

Bartholomew is a mysterious figure. He was born into a fairly wealthy family from Whitby sometime around 1120 and given the name Tostig. He grew up to be a powerful and boisterous young man, who drank rather more than was good for him and loved to cause trouble, start fights and chase women. Then, in about 1140, he was suddenly struck dumb and stood stock-still, as if transfixed. When Tostig snapped out of his state a few hours later he was a changed man. He declared that God had work for him to do, packed up a bag with some clothes and a little money and walked out of Whitby. His family heard nothing of him for years. Then Tostig turned up in Durham. He told Prior Laurence of Durham Priory that he had been to Norway, had been ordained a priest and now wished to be admitted as a monk. The man seemed to be possessed of a burning faith, changing his name to Bartholomew and spending hours on end in the church reading the Bible, studying the works of holy men and singing praises to God. Later he moved to Farne with Aelwin.

Some years after Aelwin left, another Durham monk named Thomas moved to Inner Farne. Together the two men had visions of the Devil, who came to Farne to tempt them. Bartholomew was able to drive the Devil away each time. The stories of these visits spread far and wide, attracting hordes of pilgrims and worshippers. Thomas died after a few

St Cuthbert's Spring at Bellingham. The water miraculously began to flow after St Cuthbert's coffin rested here on its long years of wandering around northern England, and is said to have remarkable healing properties.

Isolated, overgrown and ruined, the chapel of St Cuthbert at Tillmouth is an atmospheric site.

years, but Bartholomew continued to have visions of the Devil, St Cuthbert and Edulf the hermit. He died in 1193 and was buried on the island.

After Bartholomew died, the monastery at Durham took over the Inner Farne and established a regular cell of three monks. The cell was endowed with lands on the mainland to provide a modest rent to enable the monks to buy food and other necessities. In 1450, the holy nature of the island was spoilt somewhat when the English king ordered a watch tower to be built on the island from which soldiers could keep an eye open for Scottish ships heading south. In 1536 King Henry VIII closed down the monastery at Durham and confiscated the mainland estate of Farne for his own use. The last monk known to have lived on Inner Farne was John Duket who went there in 1532: what became of him is unknown.

In 1843 the ecclesiastical authorities of Durham Cathedral decided to take a hand. The chapel of St Cuthbert was restored and provision made for occasional services in praise of God to be held. They are still held, from time to time, continuing the tradition begun by St Cuthbert more than a thousand years ago.

Chapter 9

Mysterious Crimes

Northumberland has never been a particularly crime-ridden county, but that does not mean that it is entirely peaceful and safe. Every area has individuals who will take a chance now and then. Usually, of course, the combined efforts of the law-abiding majority and the police either deter the crime from occuring in the first place, or ensure that the culprits are brought swiftly to justice. However, there are several crimes in Northumberland that have gone unsolved, or about which there is some mystery as to who was responsible or why they committed the crime they did.

Take, for instance, the case of John Margetts of North Shields. In 1827 John was 16 years old and working for Dr Greenhow as a helper in the surgery, and as an errand boy and general assistant. He worked hard and was popular with both the doctor and his patients. On the night of 21 February Dr Greenhow was called out to attend Mrs Gaunt, who lived about 100 yards away and was showing symptoms of cholera. The cholera outbreak then sweeping the Tyne had meant that the good doctor had been working very hard and he was extremely tired.

At 5am Dr Greenhow got home and made up the prescription for Mrs Gaunt. He simply could not face going out again, so he awoke young John and told him to run the medicine round. Dr Greenhow then collapsed onto his bed and fell into a deep sleep. He woke up around 9am with a bitterly cold wind blowing through the house. He found the back door flapping open and no sign of young John. His coat and hat were missing, but his boots were sitting by the fire, as if placed there to dry or warm.

Dr Greenhow thought this odd, but assumed that his young helper had slipped out in his shoes on a quick errand and had failed to shut the door properly. After half an hour had passed Dr Greenhow became concerned. He walked up to Mrs Gaunt's house to ask about young John. The patient told him that the boy had delivered the medicine at around 5.30am and had then left.

Dr Greenhow then recalled that John had asked permission to have a few hours off to visit his family. Perhaps he had thought the doctor would not awaken for some hours and had taken the opportunity to slip off home. Dr Greenhow walked across town to the Margetts household. John had not been home at all. That was when Dr Greenhow, not to mention John's family, became worried.

This was in the days before an official police force, but the magistrates had teams of men ready to investigate crimes, so it was to them that Greenhow now went. The magistrates sent out men to question locals, while adverts were put in the local newspapers asking for information. This produced three leads.

The first was a man who had been walking to work along Tyne Street about 6am on the day John vanished. He said that he had heard what sounded like two men arguing in a side street. One of them had said, 'What are you doing with me?'

The second lead came from a fisherman who recalled that at around 6.30am he had seen three men walking along the quayside. At the time, the fisherman had thought one of the men to be drunk as the other two were half-carrying him along, but on reflection perhaps the 'drunk' had been dazed or concussed.

The third lead came a few days later when a landlord called on a man named Joey Aird for his rent. Aird had gone, leaving nothing behind in his small room except a torn shirt collar. Neighbours reported that Aird had left in a hurry on the morning John Margetts went missing.

A description of Aird was sent out, together with an announcement of a reward of £100, then a considerable sum, for any firm news of John Margetts. Neither Aird nor John were ever heard of again and the reward went unclaimed.

The family of Joseph Millie, unlike that of John Margetts, did find out what had happened to their relative, but nobody was ever convicted of the murder. Early on the morning of 7 December 1838 a resident of Pilgrim Street, Newcastle, spotted smoke coming from a window of the Savings Bank and called the fire brigade. The firemen were swiftly on the scene, but at first could not get into the bank, which was locked up for the night and was one of the more robust and secure buildings in the city. When they finally did get in the firemen soon found that the blaze was only a small one and quickly put it out.

Having extinguished the flames, the firemen then found a dead body lying in the office where the fire had begun. A quick inspection found that coals had been placed over the body, presumably in the hope of helping it to be consumed by flames. The head of the unfortunate man had been smashed in and a bloodstained poker lay nearby. A second body was found slumped in a corner of the room with cuts about the face and neck, but this man was breathing. The firemen hauled the man out into the fresh air and sent for a doctor.

The magistrates were called and it soon transpired that the dead man was Joseph Millie, a junior clerk at the bank, while the wounded man was Archibald Bolam, the bank's chief actuary. When Bolam was sufficiently recovered to talk he gave his version of events. He said that the day before he had received a letter at the bank making dire but unspecified threats against both himself and the bank. He had not recognised the writing, and since the threats were vague he had simply put the letter in his desk and ignored it as the ramblings of a disgruntled customer.

That night, however, he had awoken with a start. He now thought that he had found the writing familiar after all, so, he decided to slip back to the bank to compare the threatening letter with other letters that he had on file. When he arrived the doors were locked, just as he had left them. He had let himself in and walked through to his office only to discover Millie's body. Bolam said that he had turned to leave and call the authorities when he was struck from behind by a tall man with a blackened face. A fight had then ensued, which ended with Bolam losing consciousness. He had not come round, he said, until the firemen had carried him to the street.

Subsequent investigations soon turned up suspicious circumstances. The bank had closed at 3pm on the day of the murder. As the staff left, they reported that Millie had been keen to talk to Bolam and had stayed behind. The last anyone had seen of Millie was when he was entering Bolam's office.

It then turned out that Bolam, an outwardly respectable member of the church and an honest man, had huge gambling debts and was in the habit of visiting prostitutes down by the docks. It was theorised that Bolam had been fiddling money from the bank to fund his wayward lifestyle, Millie had found out about it and had been murdered by Bolam to ensure his silence. Accountants were called in but no discrepancies in the bank's affairs could be found.

With no other suspect in sight, Bolam was put on trial. The evidence against him was purely circumstantial and the judge clearly thought it so weak that his summing-up was virtually an instruction to the jury to find Bolam not guilty. In fact, the jury found him guilty of manslaughter. Bolam was sentenced to transportation to Australia, where he spent the rest of his life. When he died in 1862, Bolam left instructions that his tombstone should carry the epitaph: 'Here lies an honest man'.

Another unsolved murder took place in 1873 at Edlingham, though it is more than likely that we can now identify the killer. By this time a regular constabulary had been established in Northumberland, each man having a regular beat which he walked around to keep an eye on the people and places of his area. Thus it was, that at 3am, PC Grey was tramping along the lane just outside Edlingham.

It appears that Grey saw something suspicious in a nearby field for he climbed the fence and began walking and then running over the ploughed ground. He was then shot at close range with a shotgun, falling to the ground and dying soon after. The sound of the gunshot brought men running from the village, one of whom saw three men running off toward some nearby woods.

The police were called and searched the area. They found the boot marks of three different men in the field, together with some discarded game. Clearly, Grey had come across poachers, given chase and been killed for his devotion to duty. One of the boot marks showed a clear split along the heel.

Edlingham Castle, close to where George Edgell was arrested for poaching in 1879. Edgell was soon linked to other crimes, but mystery surrounds the extent of his guilt.

The police went out to round up all the known poachers of the area in order to inspect their boots. One Charles Richardson was found to have a boot with a cut along the heel. He was promptly arrested, along with George Edgell, a known accomplice of his. Despite the evidence of the boot mark, Edgell and Richardson walked free. There was no evidence that either of them owned a shotgun and both had witnesses who stated that they were miles away from Edlingham on the night in question.

Then, six years later, Edgell was arrested again, this time for poaching. When he was searched Edgell was found to be carrying goods that linked him to a burglary at Edlingham, in the course of which the houseowner had been shot and seriously wounded.

Realising he had no defence against either charge, Edgell decided to turn Queen's evidence and testify against his fellow burglar who had fired the almost fatal shot: none other than Charles Richardson. There can be little doubt that Richardson had also shot and killed PC Grey, though this was never proven.

Rather different was the murder of John Nisbet on 18 March 1910. A man was convicted and hanged for this crime, but mystery remains as to whether he was actually guilty. Every Friday John Nisbet left Newcastle for Widdrington by train, carrying with him a bag containing the wages for the miners of Stobswood Colliery: £370 9/6d. There was nothing at all unusual in the habit of carrying cash around like this at that time.

On this particular Friday Nisbet went to Newcastle station along with three other clerks. They then split up to catch different trains. As they did so one clerk, Charles Raven, saw Nisbet meet another man. Nisbet obviously knew the newcomer and greeted him as a friend. Raven had seen the man with Nisbet before and recognised him, but did not know his name. Nisbet and the unknown man were seen at Heaton station sitting in the carriage. However, by the time the train had reached Alnmouth, Nisbet had been found shot dead on the floor of the carriage by a porter. The bag and the money were gone.

The police were called and investigations began, while Nisbet's employers put up a reward of £100 for information on the killer. A description of the man seen with Nisbet was produced and publicised through the newspapers. People known to have been on the

Newcastle station from which bank messenger John Nisbet began his fatal journey on 18 March 1910.

train were interviewed by the police. It was quickly established that the murder had taken place between Stannington, where Nisbet and his companion had been seen, and Morpeth, by which time the compartment in which they had been travelling and where the body had been found was seen to be empty by a man walking past on the platform. It was assumed the murderer had got off at Morpeth with the money. The bag, minus the money, was later found hidden in countryside a short walk from Morpeth.

One of the men questioned said that he had seen a friend, John Dickman, on the train, but that Dickman had ignored him, which he thought odd. The police called on Dickman, who confirmed that he had been on the train. Dickman said that he had been reading a newspaper and so had missed his stop, Stannington, and had got off at Morpeth where he waited for the next train back to Stannington. Dickman resembled the description of the wanted man and had admitted getting off at Morpeth. He was duly arrested.

It soon transpired that Dickman was heavily in debt, had owned a revolver in the past and blood was found on his gloves. On the other hand, none of the stolen money was found on Dickman, he had sold his gun some time earlier and the bloodstains might have been his own from a cut that he had suffered. When the people who had seen Nisbet with the stranger were brought forward they were not entirely certain that Dickman was the right man. He looked like the man who had been seen with Nisbet, but none of them could state that they were absolutely sure.

Despite the flimsy evidence, Dickman was found guilty. He was hanged on 10 August 1910. That leaves the question of whether or not Dickman was guilty. At the time opinions were sharply divided in Northumberland. Today, it is unlikely that a jury would convict Dickman on the evidence available, and if it did the Court of Appeal would probably overturn the conviction.

On the other hand, it has since been revealed that Dickman's record was not entirely unblemished. He had never been convicted of any crime, but he had been arrested three times. The first arrest was for fraud, but the other two were both for murder. And both of those murders had involved the theft of considerable sums of money. Dickman had not been convicted of any of these crimes, and even if he were guilty of them that would still not prove that he had killed Nisbet.

The mystery remains.

INDEX OF PLACE NAMES

Aberdeen 67

Actium 78

Alnmouth 110–11, 178, 189

Alnwick 8, 42, 59, 100–02, 136, 141

Alwinton 24, 110, 112

Badon Hill 85

Balwearie 159

Bamburgh 8, 33, 75, 89–91, 93, 97, 99,
    102, 112–13, 117, 128, 167–69,
    174–75, 177

Barcombe 64

Barmoor 16

Barrasford 114–15

Belford 23, 73

Bellingham 107–09, 181, 183

Bellister 133–34

Belsay 116

Bernicia 174

Berwick 73, 152–53

Black Heddon 26–29

Blanchland 97, 98, 110, 117–20, 125

Blenkinsopp 48–51, 53, 65

Branxton 131

Bremenium 80

Brinkburn 42, 61–62, 75–76, 96–97

Callaly 34–35, 44–45, 47, 120

Camlann 86, 89

Capheaton 121

Carlisle 64, 86, 177

Catcleugh 122

Chathill 42

Chester 66, 86

Chesterholm 44

Chillingham 123–24, 164–67

Chollerford 106–07

Chollerton 107

Coalburne 20

Cockenheugh 23

Collier Heugh 64, 65

Coquetdale 9, 167

Corbridge 75, 78–79, 82–83

Craster 25, 26

Cresswell 17, 18, 124–25

Crocken Heugh 64

Derwentwater 58–59, 125–26

Dilston 58–59, 125–27

Dunstanburgh 75, 94–95, 102, 127–28

Durham 20, 61, 152–53, 182, 184

Easington 177

East Anglia 78, 85, 88, 156

Eboracum 78

Edenborough 152

Edinburgh 79

Edlingham 158–59, 162, 187–88

Ellingham 128

Elsdon 31–33, 35, 128–29

Farne Islands 8, 33, 182

Featherstone 129–30

Fentonhill 73

Fenwick 147–49

Flodden Field 131–32

Framwellgate 20

Glasgow 121

Greenwich 126

Gunnarton 59–60

Hadrian's Wall 52–53, 61, 65–66, 81–84,
    86, 142, 165, 174, 177

Haltwhistle 13, 56, 58, 133, 157

Harbottle 24

Hartington 149

Haughton 115–16

Hazelrigg 23, 26, 31, 64–65, 141

Heavenfield 90–1

Hedgeley 102, 104, 105

Hedley 20–23, 26, 31

Hexham 7, 59, 61, 65, 102, 177–78

Hilderton 177

Howick 136

Humshaugh 41

Inner Farne 34, 176, 177, 179, 181–82, 184

Inverurie 77

Iona 174, 175

Jutland 146
Kirknewton 39
Knaresdale 135
Kynelyn 85, 89–90
Lancaster 127–28
Langley 102
Liddesdale 115
Lincoln 78, 86
Lindisfarne 90–91, 135, 175–76, 178–79,
    181–82
London 66, 78, 107, 109, 119, 126
Longhorsely 37
Longwitton 169–171
Lorbottle 35, 159
Lowick 14–17
Lyham 64
Meldon 147–50, 163
Melrose 176, 181
Mons Graupius 77–78
Morpeth 37, 149, 158–61, 163, 190
Mount Badon 86
Nafferton 99–100
Nechtansmere 177
Netherwitton 37, 40, 42
Newcastle 7–9, 16, 20, 24, 28, 36, 50, 64,
    102, 105, 119, 132–33, 136–39, 141,
    147, 152–54, 156, 159–60, 186, 189
Newminster 149
Norham 167
North Shields 185
Old Bewick 72–73
Oswestry 91
Otterburn 46, 132–33, 141–42
Peterborough 14, 78
Pinkeyn Clough 130
Preston 119, 171–73

Rheged 85
Ripon 182
Rochester 80–81, 142
Rothbury 9–12, 24, 107, 173
Rothley 38
Roughting Linn 68–69, 73
Seaton Delaval 143, 150–51, 163
Sewingshields 86, 88
Shawdon 159
Shilbottle 30, 31
Simonside 9–13, 107, 167
South Charlton 141
South Tyne 7
Spindlestone Heugh 168–69
Stamford 14
Stamfordham 143
Stannington 190
Stobswood 189
Stonehenge 42, 58
Tankerville 124, 165, 167
Thorngrafton 64
Tillmouth 181, 184
Twyford 178
Tyndale 152
Tynedale 7
Tynemouth 7, 64, 75, 154
Warkworth 57–59, 144–45
Westmoreland 101, 105
Whitby 176, 182
Whittle Burn 100
Widdrington 189
Winlington Whitehouse 154
Yeavering Bell 74–75
York 75, 78–79, 85–86, 90, 93, 102,
    115–16, 128